THE
EHRMAN
NEEDLEPOINT
BOOK

THE

EHRMAN
NEEDLEPOINT
BOOK

Hugh Ehrman

INCLUDING DESIGNS BY
KAFFE FASSETT, CANDACE BAHOUTH,
AND ELIAN McCREADY

Photography by TIM HILL
Styling by ZÖE HILL

Reader's
Digest

THE READER'S DIGEST ASSOCIATION, INC.
Pleasantville, New York/Montreal

A Reader's Digest Book
Edited and produced by David & Charles Publishers
Photography by Tim Hill
Designed by Bridgewater Books Ltd.
Styling by Zöe Hill
Page make-up by Chris Lanaway

The credits and acknowledgments that appear on page 143 are
hereby made a part of this copyright page.

First published in Great Britain in 1995

Library of Congress Cataloging in Publication Data

Ehrman, Hugh.
    The Ehrman needlepoint book / Hugh Ehrman : including designs by
Kaffe Fassett, Candace Bahouth and Elian MCready : photography by Tim
Hill : styling by Zöe Hill.
        p.   cm.
    "First published in Great Britain in 1995"–T.p. verso.
    Includes index.
    ISBN 0-89577-861-0
    1. Canvas embroidery–Patterns. I. Title.
TT778.C3E2723   1996
746.44'2041–dc20   95-49970

CONTENTS

INTRODUCTION

This book gathers together some of the best new work produced by Ehrman's designers over the past two or three years. It has been a wonderful book to write because I have not been restricted to a particular design theme. I have had a free hand in choosing from across the Ehrman range and I have been allowed to select each design purely on its own merit – a rare luxury for an author – and for this I am most grateful to my publisher.

When this book was first proposed, my initial reaction was skeptical. Books produced by companies tend to look like glorified catalogs. Designers are better at writing about their own creations, and in any case, it is more interesting and personal to hear what they have to say themselves. It was a trip to our canvas manufacturers in Lancashire, England, that made me think again. We were discussing how to store the stencils for all of our old designs. To my amazement, I discovered that we had accumulated more than 400. It struck me that we had access here to some of the most interesting needlework patterns produced by some of the country's best designers over the past 15 years. Surely it would be possible to compile a worthwhile collection of contemporary work from this lot. It certainly was worth a try. Two years later, here is the result.

A book is, of course, more than just a group of designs. It gives us a chance to find out more about the designers themselves and what makes them tick. Writing this book

HUGH EHRMAN IN THE LONDON STORE, WHICH ACTS
AS A FOCUS FOR THEIR CUSTOMERS FROM ALL
OVER THE WORLD.

has reminded me of the wide variety of kits we produce, and how much thought and effort our designers put into them. Producing more than 50 new kits a year (or one a week), it is easy to lose sight of the fact that each one is a unique creation. I sometimes think we produce too many to do justice to them all. But when our designers are in full flow, it is hard to say no, and at the moment they are stitching as though possessed. Creating a book gives us the chance to stand back and take a more considered look at the designs.

The structure of the book fell happily into place. The patterns seemed to divide themselves naturally into their five groups, and the chapter headings are, I think, fairly self-explanatory. The text is intended to accompany the pictures, not to intrude on them. It moves back and forth, from the specific to the general, as it makes its way along. Whatever struck me as interesting about each particular design is what I have written about. There is background on the designers, a look at how they work, a little about the history of the source materials, and observations on color and composition. I have tried to keep things light and to let the pictures, as far as possible, do the talking. Each design is charted with the yarn quantities listed at the side. This allows colors to be changed and patterns to be altered.

When I go to international trade shows, I am always surprised to find other British companies taking pride of place: Elizabeth Bradley, Designers' Forum, Glorafilia, or

A VIEW OF THE EHRMAN STORE IN LONDON, WHERE
THE FULL RANGE OF NEEDLEPOINT DESIGNS
IS ON DISPLAY.

Primavera often outshine the local competition. There is no doubt that, in this specialized area, British design now leads the field, and few would deny that our designers have had an important part to play in this development. It gives me a tremendous thrill that their canvases should be stitched in so many countries. I think we should be proud of them and give credit where credit is due. This is a genuinely talented group of people who have given enormous pleasure to thousands of stitchers around the world. I hope this book will help to illustrate the artistic regeneration that British needlework has undergone in recent years, and that you will enjoy looking at their work as much as I have enjoyed writing about it.

I would like to extend a particularly warm welcome to all our American readers. Our kits have been available in the United States for nearly 10 years now through our distributor in New Hampshire (see page 143), and we have been delighted with the response to our catalog. We are always pleased to welcome so many Americans to our London store, where the creations shown in the catalog are exhibited. Being able to see the designs stitched up and properly displayed is helpful in terms of color and scale. This book gives us a wonderful opportunity to bring the work of British designers to an even larger audience.

Chapter One

TEXTILES

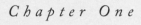

"To us pattern designers,
Persia has become a
holy-land, for there in the process of time
our art was perfected, and thence it spread to
cover for a while the world, east and west."

WILLIAM MORRIS,
THE HISTORY OF PATTERN DESIGNING

MYSORE

Annabel Nellist's wonderful design somehow captures the spirit of India. It is not necessarily the colors, composition, or subject matter. None of these alone holds the key. A combination of these factors is partly the answer, but the extra ingredient that brings the design to life is its crowded sense of Indian activity. The nature of Indian design reflects the environment of India – jostling, crowded, and often chaotic. There are people everywhere. As in life, so in art – in almost all forms of Indian textile design there is movement and event, with a host of details competing for attention. If there is one unifying feature of Indian design, it would have to be liveliness.

The great era of Indian textile art was under the Mughal emperors in the 16th century. They supervised a fusion of styles we now think of as characteristically Indian. The Mughals, who ruled India from the 16th to the 18th centuries, were descendants of the Mongols, who had controlled Asia from east to west a few centuries earlier. With their arrival, India was opened up to influences from China, Afghanistan, and Persia.

It was this rich, polyglot tradition that attracted Annabel. She has chosen an unusual mixture of architecture and pattern as the subjects for her pillow cover. This surprising combination succeeds because of her sure sense of scale. The central focus of windows and roofs anchors the design, which is further stabilized by a thin but strong geometric border. Through its patchwork technique, the overall effect becomes more textural and less pictorial. No area of color or pattern is allowed to dominate, and as a result there is a calm sense of balance amid the profusion of details.

AN INDIAN PATCHWORK IN WARM, CLEAN
COLORS FROM ANNABEL NELLIST. THE COPIOUS
DETAIL CREATES THE INTEREST, YET THE COMPOSITION
IS SO WELL BALANCED THAT THE OVERALL DESIGN
LOOKS QUITE RESTRAINED.

Maybe this design will inspire you to try your own needlework collage. Annabel's is a sophisticated and original design, but yours doesn't have to be so complicated. If you start with the regularity of a patchwork quilt, you can then let discord creep in slowly! Kaffe Fassett sometimes develops his geometric designs by playing around with groups of objects – buttons, pieces of fabric, or whatever – and then seeing what patterns they fall into. I have always thought a patchwork approach to needlepoint design has tremendous possibilities. You don't need to be a great draftsman or figurative drawer. You can start with a few relatively simple motifs and let color and pattern do the rest. I like the way Annabel places her skyline of buildings against a backdrop of pattern. Collage is a wonderful way of superimposing unexpected images, and it is great fun.

CANVAS: 12-gauge

STITCH: Half-cross or continental

DESIGN AREA: 18 × 15 inches

YARN: Anchor tapisserie or Paternayan

Shade	Anchor	Paternayan	
Flame	8204	940	5 skeins
Cream	8006	263	7 skeins
Rose Pink	8400	931	5 skeins
Ancient Blue	8744	570	4 skeins
Autumn Gold	8060	732	3 skeins
Cinnamon	9384	443	8 skeins
Ocean Blue	8838	531	2 skeins
Gobelin Green	8882	532	3 skeins
Cherry Red	8220	900	5 skeins
Maize	8040	753	2 skeins

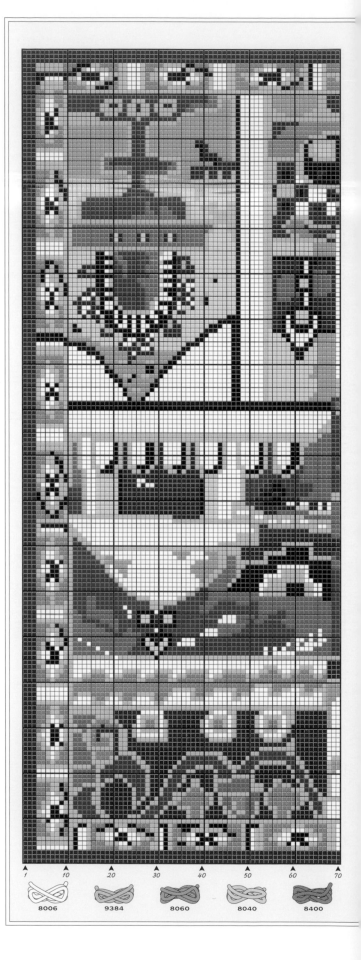

80   90   100   110   120   130   140   150   160   170   180   190   200   210 214

8204   8220   8882   8838   8744

JAIPUR STRIPE

We move on to Annabel Nellist's next Indian design, "Jaipur Stripe." Many of the colors are the same, but there is a noticeable addition of green, which alters the overall color balance. Here Annabel uses thin strips of patchwork pattern vertically, whereas the patchwork skyline of "Mysore" was constructed on the horizontal, and the association with Eastern textiles is even more direct. The small areas of color are interesting to work but not difficult. The blocks of color may be small, but they are clearly defined, avoiding the complexity of gradual shading found in many of our kits.

I am sure one of the reasons this design has proven so popular is that it is easy to live with. Interior design goes through its cycles like everything else, and Indian design has been in the ascendant lately, but a pattern like "Jaipur Stripe" is perennial. It looks comfortable in a variety of settings, from the traditional and stately to the cleanest, most open contemporary spaces. It could be argued that Persian and Eastern carpets have generally proven to be one of the most enduring constants of European interiors. For six or seven centuries, these carpets have been found on the floors, or earlier on the tables, of European houses. Architectural styles and tastes in furniture have come and gone. Fashions in fabrics, paint colors, and wallpapers have evolved, along with the scale and use of rooms, but the Eastern carpet remains. And it remains, like a rock of ages, largely unaltered. The same carpet looks as fitting on the table in a Holbein painting as it does on the floor of a 1990's New York apartment. You would not be surprised to find an Eastern carpet in any home, old or new, and the same goes for Annabel Nellist's "Jaipur Stripe." Her use of pattern is different, her motifs and colors distinctive, but in essence this pillow remains in the tradition of Eastern carpet design.

Annabel has dotted birds and architectural motifs over the pattern in a delightfully random manner. This is a common feature of Indian embroidery. Embroidered quilts, called *kanthas,* are made throughout Bengal by all castes of women, both Hindu and Muslim. The patterns and figures – often birds and animals – have symbolic significance, as they did for Elizabethan embroiderers. Their placing and coloring are entirely a matter for the individual embroiderer. As a result, no two *kanthas* are alike, and they are infused with the spontaneity typical of folk art around the world. Annabel adopts this style with her birds all facing in different directions. Combined with her balanced but asymmetric use of pattern, her design has a truly Indian flavor.

Another designer who has always appreciated that the vitality of Eastern design lies in its irregularity is Kaffe Fassett. There are none of his carpet-inspired designs in this book, but those of you who are familiar with his work will know what I mean. He always keeps his outlines rough to capture the authentic, human feel of handmade textiles. It often surprises me how few textile designers see the importance of this. So many of the kilim patterns around at the moment look dead. The reason is simple: they have neat, straight lines and regular repeats. Stitched geometric patterns come alive when things start to go wrong! Or to put it more soberly, the eye is caught by a different outline or a dash of color appearing unexpectedly. This personalizes the design, adding a new layer of depth to the pattern. Embroidery, being free-form and not subject to any mechanical restrictions, allows for such an approach. That is why it has the potential for being the most creative of all the textile arts. It is an advantage that gives the stitcher far greater freedom of expression than the weaver, block printer, or fabric designer.

ANNABEL NELLIST IS A TEXTILE DESIGNER BY TRAINING, AND THIS IS EVIDENT IN HER NEEDLEWORK. SHE HAS ALSO PRODUCED CARDS, BOOKMARKS, AND OTHER TYPES OF STATIONERY, BUT HER STYLE IS PARTICULARLY WELL SUITED TO FABRICS.

Annabel has recently adapted this design for a rug, and it works well. She uses a 12-gauge canvas here to capture the detail, but you could enlarge this design by transferring it onto a 10-gauge canvas. Many people prefer larger pillows, and these Eastern textile patterns are particularly suitable. If you use a 10-gauge canvas, the finished pillow will measure $21\frac{1}{2} \times 18$ inches, which is a comfortable size for sinking into. You need to be careful about using different canvas sizes. There is usually a good reason why a designer has chosen a particular gauge. Many designs would look crude if they were simply enlarged in this way, but there is enough detail in "Jaipur Stripe" to justify it in this case. It is also a question of scale. The largest single motif or block of color is probably the bird in the bottom right-hand corner, which is not very big. Because no particular section of pattern predominates, an increase in the overall size of roughly 20 percent will not look odd or alter the character of the design. Either way, working from the chart gives you the chance to choose your own size.

CANVAS: 12-gauge

STITCH: Half-cross or continental

DESIGN AREA: 18 × 15 inches

YARN: Paternayan

Shade	Paternayan	
Caramel	442	5 skeins
Honey Yellow	732	2 skeins
Honey Yellow	734	3 skeins
Gray	202	1 skein
Deep Blue	570	3 skeins
Peacock Green	520	4 skeins
Peacock Green	521	2 skeins
Pine Green	662	2 skeins
Cream	263	3 skeins
Fawn	444	3 skeins
Cherry Red	840	4 skeins
Old Rose	D211	3 skeins
Damson	920	4 skeins
Khaki	453	3 skeins

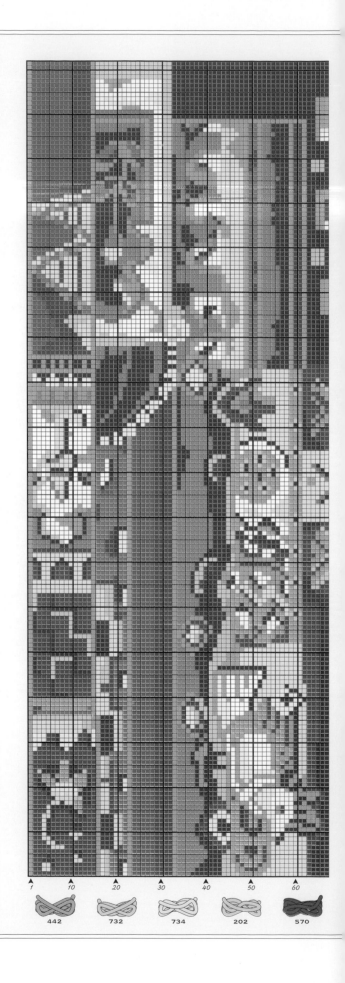

| 70 | 80 | 90 | 100 | 110 | 120 | 130 | 140 | 150 | 160 | 170 | 180 | 190 | 200 | 210 |

| 520 | 521 | 662 | 263 | 444 | 840 | D211 | 920 | 453 |

THE OWL

All of the designs in this first chapter were inspired by or are based on textile patterns. But stylistically that is all that links this eclectic group, which illustrates the enormous breadth and variety of textile design around the world. We now jump with dramatic contrast from India to England in the 1880's and the work of William Morris.

William Morris has to be the best known and best loved British textile designer of that century. In recent years we have seen far too many Morris-style pastiches gracing everything from tea towels and needlepoint kits to T-shirts and mugs. Yet despite this unrelenting saturation, the appeal of his work remains as strong as ever. In 1980 Ehrman, in association with the Royal School of Needlework, produced a kit called "Victorian Bird." We incorrectly ascribed it to William Morris. This stirred up a hornet's nest, generating a furious correspondence from Morris fans pointing out our error. The kit also sold like hot cakes. It was a reasonable enough design, but there is no doubt the magic name of William Morris acted like a talisman for needleworkers. This episode opened my eyes to the extent of Morris's following. His appeal endures because he produced so much of quality, and there is still work of his to be rediscovered. When Neil McCallum showed me his painted canvas of "The Owl," I was amazed I had not seen this particular design before.

This design is based on one of Morris's woven tapestries, which were heavily influenced by Flemish verdure pieces. Perhaps the best known of this group was "The Woodpecker," produced in 1885. William Morris's most successful tapestry designs were collaborations with Burne-Jones. But John Henry Dearle made an overlooked contribution, and an important one. Dearle had started as an assistant at the Oxford Street store in London but soon developed his own strong ideas on design. He designed many of the backgrounds for Morris's tapestries and was responsible for the familiar flowing floral patterns, which he adapted from 17th-century Italian silks.

Neil McCallum has quite rightly used a fine mesh of canvas for this hanging. It does, however, use a lot of yarn. This panel is a very practical shape; there are few homes that would have difficulty finding a place for it. Neil is now working on its companion for our next catalog.

CANVAS: 13-gauge

STITCH: Half-cross or continental

DESIGN AREA: 32 × 19½ inches

YARN: Appleton tapestry yarn or Paternayan

Shade	Appleton	Paternayan	
Iron Gray	965	200	2 skeins
Honeysuckle Yellow	692	754	8 skeins
Honeysuckle Yellow	695	732	9 skeins
Autumn Yellow	476	722	5 skeins
Sea Green	407	660	49 skeins
Rose Pink	759	900	3 skeins
Kingfisher	488	580	3 skeins
Sky Blue	564	584	3 skeins
Sky Blue	562	555	2 skeins
Grass Green	254	692	2 skeins
Early English Green	542	653	3 skeins
Purple	105	311	1 skein
Rose Pink	755	D275	5 skeins
Olive Green	243	642	4 skeins
Golden Brown	903	442	2 skeins
Dull Rose Pink	146	910	2 skeins
Bright Rose Pink	941	934	3 skeins
Purple	103	312	2 skeins
Pastel Lilac	885	313	1 skein
Red Fawn	305	400	1 skein
Autumn Yellow	478	721	1 skein
Chocolate	183	453	2 skeins
Chocolate	184	432	2 skeins
Turquoise	524	D502	2 skeins
Turquoise	526	D501	2 skeins

HENRY DEARLE WORKED FOR WILLIAM MORRIS, BUT THIS
WAS VERY MUCH HIS OWN DESIGN. IT WAS WORKED IN SILKS
ON A WOVEN SILK DAMASK GROUND, AROUND 1890.

965

692

695

476

407

759

488

564

562

254

542

105

755

243   903   146   941   103   885   305   478   183   184   524   526

MAYTIME

I t is highly appropriate that we should retrace our steps from William Morris to the world of medieval tapestry. In Morris's opinion, the medieval and Gothic period, up to about 1500, represented the high watermark for tapestry design. From the 14th century, tapestry was clearly seen as one of the major decorative arts. Despite the decline in church hangings (due to larger windows and more space for tombs), the workshops of Brussels, Arras, and Tournai were fully occupied, providing made-to-order hangings for castles and large homes throughout Europe. It is a period that has fascinated Candace Bahouth for years, and in terms of needlework design, she has made it her own.

Candace's book, *Medieval Needlepoint* (1993), is a pageant of richly patterned ornament, symbol, and emblem. Lions, unicorns, fleur-de-lis, heraldry, and the constellations crowd the pages. Her colors epitomize the period – dense and sumptuous burgundies, royal blue, raspberry pink, and gold. The woven hangings from which she takes her inspiration rejoice in the regenerative magic of nature, their backgrounds filled with field upon field of individual flowers. The example that springs most immediately to mind is the series of the "Lady with Unicorn" in the Cluny Museum in Paris, and it was this series that inspired Candace's "Rug of Flowers," which can be seen pictured with "Maytime" on pages 26 and 27.

Candace's millefleur patterns faithfully reproduce the sinuous, elongated elegance of medieval embroidered flowers. Lesser copies are always too squat. She arranges the flowers to form a balanced picture, while taking equal care to balance her colors. To maintain the movement and informality of the design, she lets the odd leaf overlap the border. Her borders have a very personal stamp to them, and this one is no exception. The four sides are all different – no mirror

CANDACE BAHOUTH HAS MADE A NAME FOR HERSELF
WITH HER MEDIEVAL DESIGNS. HER KNOWLEDGE AND LOVE
OF THE PERIOD ARE SELF-EVIDENT.

images here – and although motifs recur, their spacing and coalition vary from side to side. This, in turn, adds to the rug's vitality in a subtle, yet essential way. Many other designers would have structured this border more formally and would have lost much of the rug's liveliness as a result. Candace's simple, effective use of color, combining burgundy and gold, shows what restrained good taste is all about, and to my eye, the scale and balance of this composition could not be improved upon.

"Maytime," with its similar border, coloring, and floral theme, was designed to go with the "Rug of Flowers." It is a lovely pillow in its own right and has proven one of Candace's most popular.

Candace's borders are wonderful. It would be possible to use this one to make a photograph or mirror frame. We have never produced kits for frames because everyone wants a different size, but a chart allows you to adapt the pattern yourself. Kaffe Fassett had a lovely lichen-patterned frame in *Glorious Needlepoint*, and Mary Norden had a number in her last book, *Mary Norden's Needlepoint*.

This chart also illustrates Candace's skill with backgrounds. She rarely uses a single matte color. By mixing two close, complementary colors, she re-creates the faded, weathered look of older textiles. For those of you who stitch your own designs, here is a good example of how to achieve this effect with relative simplicity. But make sure when you mix your two sets of color that you do so randomly; otherwise, you could produce a regular pattern.

CANVAS: 10-gauge

STITCH: Half-cross or continental

DESIGN AREA: 16 × 16 inches

YARN: Appleton tapestry yarn or Paternayan

Shade	Appleton	Paternayan	
Dull Rose Pink	142	923	1 skein
Medium Blue	157	531	6 skeins
Medium Blue	158	531	6 skeins
Flame Red	209	D211	6 skeins
Bright Terracotta	225	931	4 skeins
Jacobean Green	292	603	2 skeins
Sea Green	401	613	3 skeins
Autumn Yellow	472	703	1 skein
Honeysuckle Yellow	694	733	4 skeins
Bright China Blue	743	561	1 skein
Rose Pink	755	D275	1 skein
Royal Blue	821	543	1 skein
Heraldic Gold	841	704	1 skein
Custard Yellow	851	D541	1 skein
Pastel Cream	882	263	1 skein
Golden Brown	903	442	6 skeins
Bright Rose Pink	947	902	1 skein
Drab Fawn	954	453	1 skein
Rust	994	852	1 skein

1 10 20 30 40 50 60 70 80 90 100 110 120 130 140 150 159

142 158 225 401 694 755 851 882 947 994

157 209 292 472 743 821 841 903 954

OVERLEAF: THE "RUG OF FLOWERS" PROVIDED

THE INSPIRATION AND MATERIAL FOR A PAIR OF

MATCHING PILLOWS, OF WHICH "MAYTIME" HAS

PROVED THE MOST POPULAR.

BERLIN
ROSES

We end this chapter with a look at Berlin Woolwork patterns of the 1860's. This design is based squarely and directly on the stitched textiles of that time, and the actual pattern charts of the day formed the basis of the design.

Three years ago we were approached by Sotheby's, who had a miscellaneous collection of Berlin Woolwork charts in one of their forthcoming sales. They wondered if we would be interested in buying them by private arrangement in advance of the auction. I was intrigued and went along to have a look. On the whole, these high-Victorian charted patterns are not really our scene. They tend to consist of pastoral landscapes – shepherds set in bucolic idylls, children with pets, tight little compositions of birds and fruits, and suffocating excesses with cabbage roses. In this assortment of charted patterns, however, one feature stood out: whoever put them together knew how to draw. These charts have a static, three-dimensional stillness to them. The stereoscopic clarity is achieved by using a very fine graph paper (24 squares to the inch or finer), lots of colors for shading, and a rigorous application of scientific proportion when dealing with leaves and flowers. The effect is eerie, but rather fascinating. It struck me that we could extract different sections and create our own patterns using existing elements from within the designs. David Merry, who has great experience at producing needlework charts, was the obvious choice for the job, and he set about his task with relish. He changed, amalgamated, and repositioned until the "Berlin Roses" emerged – a hybrid construct of contemporary and 1860's design. We then stitched it in paler, fresher colors to maintain a more contemporary feel, and I think it turned out very well.

The Berlin Woolwork charts used, on average, more thsan 30 colors. The maximum number of colors we can print is around 25, so David also had to simplify the colors without losing the detailed shading of the originals. Here again he has done an excellent job.

This style of needlework became known as Berlin Woolwork because the early charts were produced by two Berlin print sellers, Mme. Wittich and Herr Philipson, who commissioned embroidery designs for reproduction on graph paper. They became popular for two reasons. Groups of women could stitch and chat at the same time, making needlework a more social activity, and by the technical needle-

work standards of the day, they were relatively easy. In a way, they were the precursors of the printed kits of today, and they sold in large numbers. After the success of "Berlin Roses," we were bitten by the bug and are now producing a series along the same lines. The second one that David designed for us can be seen in the final chapter.

IN NEEDLEWORK, IT SEEMS, THE ROSE SHALL NEITHER WITHER NOR FADE. IT IS A PERENNIAL, REDISCOVERED BY SUCCEEDING GENERATIONS OF STITCHERS.

1 10 20 30 40 50 60 70 80 90 100 110 120 130

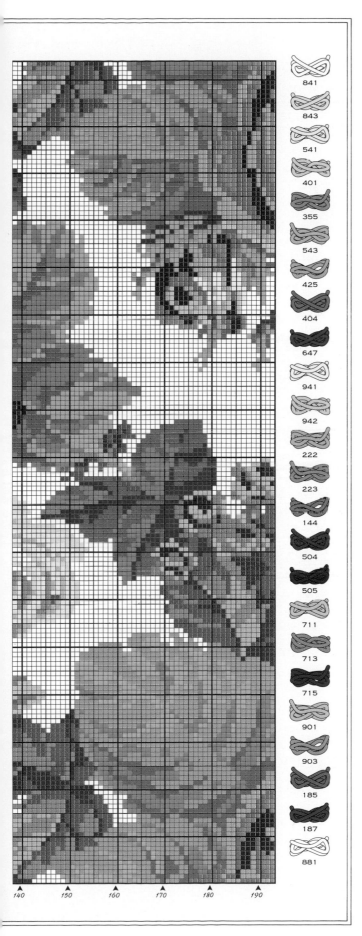

This design is ideal for choosing your own background color. We have suggested a couple of options. Another idea for background coloring is to use two contrasting tones, and to apply them to different sections of the background. In the design there are basically five areas of background color that are stitched in blocks. Try alternating each of these blocks in cream or charcoal gray. It sounds alarming but looks very stylish. Or to achieve an antique look, stitch the background area mixing two tones of your chosen color. Stitching in this speckled, random manner will give a much richer, textural quality to the pattern.

CANVAS: 12-gauge

STITCH: Half-cross or continental

DESIGN AREA: 14 × 15 inches

YARN: Appleton tapestry yarn or Paternayan

Shade	Appleton	Paternayan	
Heraldic Gold	841	704	5 skeins
Heraldic Gold	843	733	1 skein
Early English Green	541	644	1 skein
Sea Green	401	613	1 skein
Gray Green	355	603	4 skeins
Early English Green	543	693	3 skeins
Leaf Green	425	621	3 skeins
Sea Green	404	611	3 skeins
Peacock Blue	647	660	2 skeins
Bright Rose Pink	941	934	1 skein
Bright Rose Pink	942	933	1 skein
Bright Terracotta	222	933	2 skeins
Bright Terracotta	223	D275	1 skein
Dull Rose Pink	144	912	1 skein
Scarlet	504	950	1 skein
Scarlet	505	940	2 skeins
Wine Red	711	914	1 skein
Wine Red	713	912	1 skein
Wine Red	715	910	1 skein
Golden Brown	901	443	2 skeins
Golden Brown	903	442	2 skeins
Chocolate	185	431	2 skeins
Chocolate	187	430	2 skeins

Background (choose one color)

Pastel Cream	881	262	1 hank
Scarlet	504	950	1 hank

31

TEXTILES

Chapter Two
~

THE
SEA

"Of all the objects I have seen,
there is none which affects my
imagination so much as the sea or ocean.
I cannot see the heaving of this prodigious
bulk of water, even in a calm, without a
pleasing astonishment."

JOSEPH ADDISON'S
ESSAY ON THE SEA IN THE *SPECTATOR*, 1712

ROMAN MOSAIC

I originally started in business with my brother Richard and, together with our needlepoint kits company, we ran a gallery specializing in modern craft design from silversmithing to ceramics. In those days needlepoint was an artistic backwater. Kaffe Fassett had been asked by a newspaper to design a needlepoint kit for a reader offer and the scale of its success took everyone by surprise. He was convinced that there was an untapped market for different needlework design that was waiting to be developed, and it was he who talked Richard and I into producing needlepoint kits. Our policy has always been to bring new designers into the world of needlework and this policy is in keeping with the spirit of the original gallery. Like Kaffe we were convinced that all this craft needed was an injection of design flair, and being in touch with so many talented designers from different disciplines was a huge advantage.

Our kits have always emphasized design rather that technique and we have never advocated complicated stitches. There is enough complexity in the patterns without adding a variety of surface textures. When we started, the market was polarized between hand-painted and very expensive canvases at one end, and cheap kits at the other. Not only was there a design gap in the middle, there was also a price gap and, along with other British needlepoint companies, we have been trying to fill it ever since. Many of those who purchase our kits will move on to designing their own canvases and this is all part of keeping the art of needlepoint alive.

Ten or 20 years ago in Britain, needlework was perceived as a genteel, fading pastime that by the turn of the century would be virtually extinct. But as the years have gone by, our customers have become younger. It is not only a question of design, it is also the nature of the craft. It is exactly the sort of activity suited to a future world of fragmented work, where those with time look for some form of artistic fulfillment. As long as the visual content remains innovative and exciting, needlework should appeal to a new generation of stitchers. It is a great way to unwind, and many of our younger customers comment on the therapeutic nature of stitching our kits. Needlework is not a fashion industry, but it does need to move with the times. This chapter reflects that approach, and I think you will find that nearly all the designs here have a fresher, cleaner, more contemporary feel to them.

As an island nation, the British have always had a fascination with the sea. How odd, then, that aquatic images feature so rarely in British needlework design. Might this have something to do with the nature of the sea? The boundless deep has a mesmeric quality, but it is dangerous. All maritime people have a healthy respect for the sea. The great descriptions of storm and tempest in the writings of Conrad, Dickens, Byron, or Tennyson are descriptions of a primeval force beyond human control. The reassuring images of pastoral life or historical allegory have, in the past, been psychologically better suited to a sedate and domestic pastime like needlework. Maybe I am wrong about this – it is only an idea – but I find it interesting that, according to Christie's auction house, views of calm waters always sell best in maritime art sales. In any case, the sea affords a wealth of decorative possibilities for the stitcher, most of them largely unexplored. Shells appear in needlework, but fish, amphibians, ships, or waves hardly ever do.

Helen Townley saw a picture of a Roman tile in a Christie's catalog and was inspired to turn it into a needlepoint. Her colors are soft and catch the movement and shading of her subject. Most fish slither by in subdued blends of neutrals – or at least they do in the cooler waters familiar to the Roman world – and, rather surprisingly, that is why she needed so many colors for such a "colorless" design. The tile needed little adaptation to become a pillow cover. When Helen saw it, she felt the shape, composition, and scale were perfect unaltered, and her skill has been in transcribing the original ceramic colors into needlework.

HELEN TOWNLEY'S ROMAN TILE PATTERN CAME TO US,
UNSOLICITED THROUGH THE MAIL. IT IS VERY RARE FOR SUCH
QUALITY TO ARRIVE IN THIS WAY, AND TAKING ADVANTAGE OF OUR
WINDFALL, WE PUT IT STRAIGHT INTO PRODUCTION.

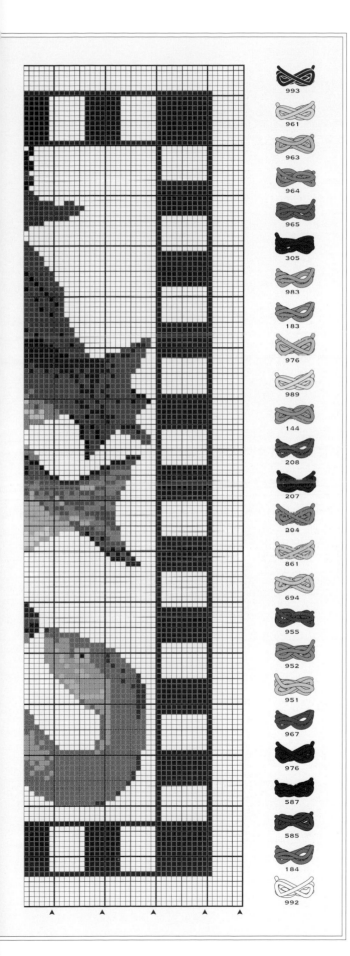

Personally, I'm not crazy about the border; I find it a little heavy. You could leave it out completely or stitch a simpler geometric border on a smaller scale or in softer colors. An alternative background could be black, or even a deep sea blue would provide enough contrast. This is a good chart to use as a design source.

CANVAS: 10-gauge

STITCH: Half-cross or continental

DESIGN AREA: 16 × 16 inches

YARN: Appleton tapestry yarn or Paternayan

Shade	Appleton	Paternayan	
Black	993	220	6 skeins
Iron Gray	961	204	1 skein
Iron Gray	963	202	1 skein
Iron Gray	964	201	1 skein
Iron Gray	965	200	1 skein
Red Fawn	305	400	1 skein
Putty Grounding	983	463	1 skein
Putty Grounding	989	246	1 skein
Dull Rose Pink	144	912	1 skein
Flame Red	207	870	2 skeins
Flame Red	208	870	1 skein
Flame Red	204	485	1 skein
Coral	861	855	1 skein
Honeysuckle Yellow	694	733	1 skein
Drab Fawn	955	452	1 skein
Drab Fawn	952	453	1 skein
Drab Fawn	951	454	1 skein
Iron Gray	967	200	2 skeins
Elephant Gray	976	461	1 skein
Elephant Gray	971	463	1 skein
Brown Grounding	587	421	1 skein
Brown Grounding	585	421	1 skein
White	992	263	17 skeins
Chocolate	184	432	1 skein
Chocolate	183	453	1 skein

NOTE: This chart design differs very slightly from that available in kit form.

CRAB AND LOBSTER

The geometric backdrops to Kaffe Fassett's "Crab" and "Lobster" are bold and dramatic, and illustrative of his gutsy approach to design at its best. He loves to experiment, not only with new color combinations but also with new subjects for needlework. It comes as no surprise that he should have chosen lobsters and crabs. These two splendid creatures were originally stitched together as a pair for a shoulder bag in his book *Glorious Needlepoint*. The checkerboard background of the bag, reminiscent of tiles at fish markets, was suggested by Steve

Lovi, the photographer. For these two pillows Kaffe has added touches of mustard, brown, and lilac to soften the harsh black and white of the backdrop, and they add a new depth. These off-colors have an almost 1950's flavor to them. On the other hand, if you prefer the crisp clarity of black and white, the chart allows you to stitch them in this way. Kaffe's shading of the lobster and crab is superb and serves as a shining example of how effectively a good artist can work with a limited number of yarns. Looking at them, you would think that at least 20 colors were used in each. Kaffe purposely restricted himself to around 10 per crustacean to keep the cost of the kits down. No other needlework designer could have shaded as subtly with so few colors, and no other needlework designer could have stitched the shells with such precision.

I HAD ALWAYS ADMIRED THE CRAB AND LOBSTER ON KAFFE FASSETT'S SHOULDER BAG IN *GLORIOUS NEEDLEPOINT,* AND AFTER SO MANY YEARS I SUGGESTED WE SHOULD LOOK AT THEM AGAIN. THE RESULT IS THIS IMAGINATIVE PAIR OF PILLOWS. BOTH THE "LOBSTER" AND THE "CRAB" ILLUSTRATE KAFFE'S INIMITABLE SKILL AT SHADING. THESE ARE THE WORKS OF A TRUE ARTIST.

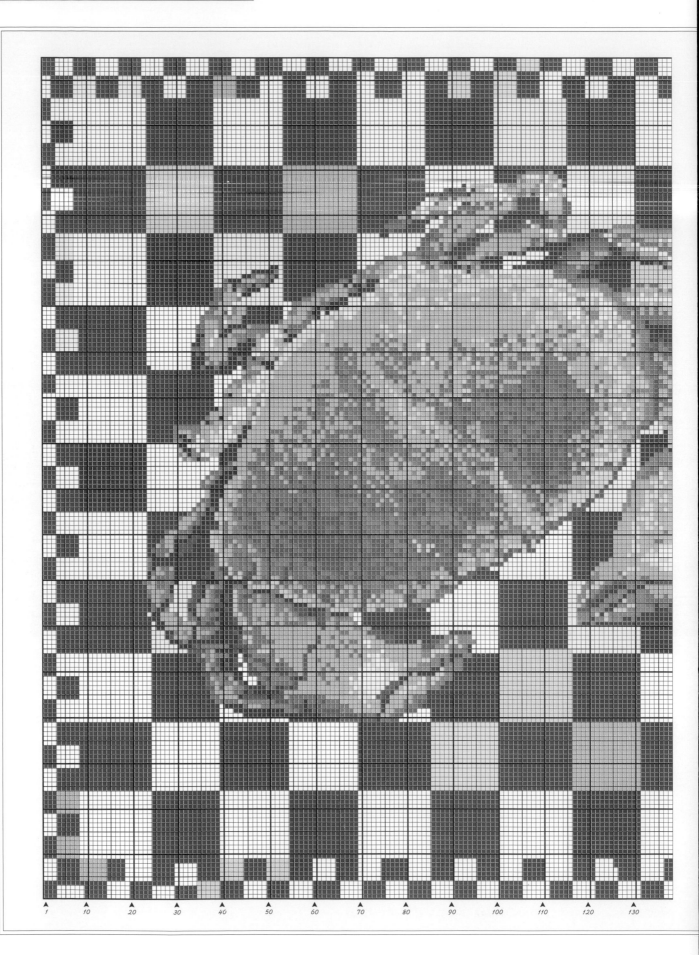

1   10   20   30   40   50   60   70   80   90   100   110   120   130

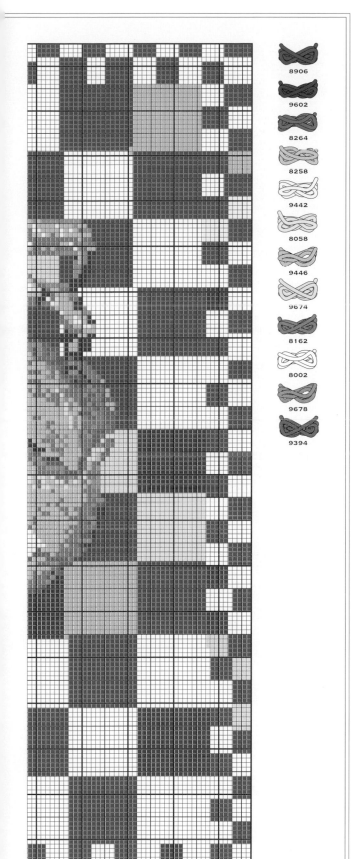

8906
9602
8264
8258
9442
8058
9446
9674
8162
8002
9678
9394

140   150   160   170   180   187

Both the crab and the lobster would look wonderful on plain-colored backgrounds. I would love to see them stitched on black. Their warm colors and the delicacy of Kaffe's shading would shine out from a deep, neutral background. They would look as striking as his individual fruits series did when stitched on bottle green. If they were on a single-colored background, they could even be used for chair cushions (how about sitting on a crab?). They could be stitched together in alternate squares to make a rug, or you could revert to Kaffe's original idea by using them for a shoulder bag – one on each side. Or just take one and use it repeatedly: a rug of crabs all crawling in different directions could be interesting. These are just a few ideas for what you could do with these dramatic images.

CANVAS: 10-gauge

STITCH: Half-cross or continental

DESIGN AREA: $17^{1}/_{2} \times 18$ inches

YARN: Anchor tapisserie or Paternayan

Shade	Anchor	Paternayan	
Sea Green	8906	660	9 skeins
Mahogany	9602	860	3 skeins
Terracotta	8264	861	2 skeins
Terracotta	8258	863	3 skeins
Nutmeg	9442	886	2 skeins
Autumn Gold	8058	804	1 skein
Nutmeg	9446	413	3 skeins
Mink	9674	D133	2 skeins
Rust Orange	8162	851	3 skeins
White	8002	261	7 skeins
Mink	9678	D123	2 skeins
Cinnamon	9394	440	1 skein

These pillows show how clever Kaffe is with simple geometric borders. The two thin strips of smaller squares have a soft, speckled feel, like confetti. This is a very simple way to soften the geometric regularity of the main background, and by echoing the central colors (but in an irregular manner), he softens the design further still. Most borders enclose; this one drifts the pattern outward. By doing so, it focuses the eye firmly on the lobster and adds to the three-dimensional quality of the design. The pillow looks like it is spilling over the edge, with the lobster walking on top. It is a small touch but integral to the design's success.

CANVAS: 10-gauge

STITCH: Half-cross or continental

DESIGN AREA: 18 × 18 inches

YARN: Anchor tapisserie or Paternayan

Shade	Anchor	Paternayan	
Mahogany	9602	860	3 skeins
Sea Green	8906	660	13 skeins
Terracotta	8264	861	2 skeins
Cinnamon	9382	465	6 skeins
Paprika	8234	862	3 skeins
Rust Orange	8162	851	4 skeins
Sand	9524	803	2 skeins
Flame Red	8196	821	4 skeins
Salmon Pink	8306	864	2 skeins
White	8002	261	8 skeins
Oak Brown	9402	445	1 skein

60   70   80   90   100   110   120   130   140   150   160   170   180 185

SEASHELL VEST

I think there can be very little doubt that Kaffe Fassett is the most varied and interesting needlework designer of our times. The color blends in some of his knitting are wonderful, his wallpapers are distinctive, and his new rag rugs look interesting. I personally think some of the fabric designs for Britain's Designers' Guild are among his best work, but it is in his needlework that so many skills come together: his draftsmanship and natural facility at drawing, his unique color sense, and his use of yarn as the chosen medium for his own brand of painting. Four or five years ago this claim would have been extravagant, but the body of work that he has now produced makes such a claim more credible. No one else has produced such a range of design in this field since William Morris – certainly not in Great Britain. I really can think of no one from the intervening years who could make such a claim. You may love his work or you may hate it, but his significance as a textile designer is indisputable.

Kaffe is the only living needlework designer with a truly international following. When 107,000 people pay to see an exhibition of his work in Stockholm, it is clear that his international following is substantial. The scope and scale of his work are unparalleled. In the 16 years we have worked with him, he has produced nearly 150 pillow covers, 10 large carpets, rugs, and hanging panels, and numerous smaller eyeglass case, slipper, shoulder bag, and chair cushion kits. He stitches these himself with the help of one or two trusted assistants. During that same period he has produced more than 50 highly detailed commissioned pieces

KAFFE FASSETT, WHO DESIGNED THE FIRST
EHRMAN NEEDLEPOINT KIT, IS STILL THE PRINCIPAL DESIGNER,
CONTRIBUTING MORE THAN 10 NEW DESIGNS TO THE
EHRMAN RANGE EVERY YEAR.

using as many as 100 colors in each, ranging from large pieces of furniture to delicately stitched vests. And all of this while simultaneously designing knitwear for Rowan, ranges of wallpapers and fabrics for Designers' Guild, writing seven books,

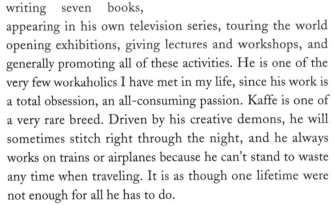

appearing in his own television series, touring the world opening exhibitions, giving lectures and workshops, and generally promoting all of these activities. He is one of the very few workaholics I have met in my life, since his work is a total obsession, an all-consuming passion. Kaffe is one of a very rare breed. Driven by his creative demons, he will sometimes stitch right through the night, and he always works on trains or airplanes because he can't stand to waste any time when traveling. It is as though one lifetime were not enough for all he has to do.

With such a prodigious output, produced at such torrential speed, quality will inevitably vary. Some artists – Picasso, Rowlandson, or Pugin being obvious, august examples – work at an explosive pace and are unconcerned with self-editing, while others refine and perfect, more conscious of the critical gaze of history. These are grand examples, but they illustrate a general split among artists, at all levels of ability, in how they approach their work. Kaffe is firmly in the former tradition and is interested in everything that he produces. His work is like a diary. However, looking at the body of his work as a whole, I am astonished how few duds there have been. Although his work is often experimental, his standards are high, and the rare Kaffe Fassett dud would stand comparison with the better efforts of many lesser designers. At some point in the future, a retrospective exhibition of his work will be mounted, edited down to the really good examples of his various styles, and it will show that he is, without question, the foremost needlework designer of our age.

I spoke of the range of his design. He has a voracious appetite for novel source material and he is usually the first with a new theme: Eastern textiles, vegetables, fruits, faces, farmyard animals, fans, and shells were all originally his ideas for commercial needlepoint kits. Nearly all of these themes have been subsequently taken up by other needlepoint kit companies. This has never worried Kaffe because he hates to repeat himself and is always moving on to the next subject. It is part of his generous nature that he has always regarded imitation as flattery. Few would deny that in this field he sets the pace. In any case, nearly all these subjects have appeared in older tapestries or embroideries anyway. The fact is that Kaffe is simply more imaginative in his plundering of the past than his more timid imitators. And once he gets an idea, it becomes his own, a good example of this being his series of stitched shells.

Over the past few years, Kaffe has stitched a shell and turtle rug, a shell pillow, and his shell-covered vest, seen here. All of these are featured in his own book, published in the fall of 1995. I am most grateful to him for allowing me to include the "Seashell Vest" in this book too. I felt that no chapter on the sea would be complete without at least one example of his shell patterns, and it is particularly nice to have a vest for a change. The kit comes with two canvases, for the left- and right-hand sides, printed for one size only. To change the fit, you need to vary the width of material at the back to suit your size. This works well, and the only thing to look out for is whether or not the overall length of the vest will be correct. The vest is edged with piping to provide the buttonholes. I love the way the shells blend into the sand, and you need to stand back to see their outlines clearly emerge. Shell slippers are following next, which should be fun.

THE FIRST VEST KIT WE PRODUCED. SOME OF KAFFE'S COMMISSIONED VESTS ARE BREATHTAKING, AND A SERIES OF THEM WERE RECENTLY PHOTOGRAPHED FOR GREETING CARDS. THEY ARE AMONG HIS FINEST NEEDLEPOINT DESIGNS.

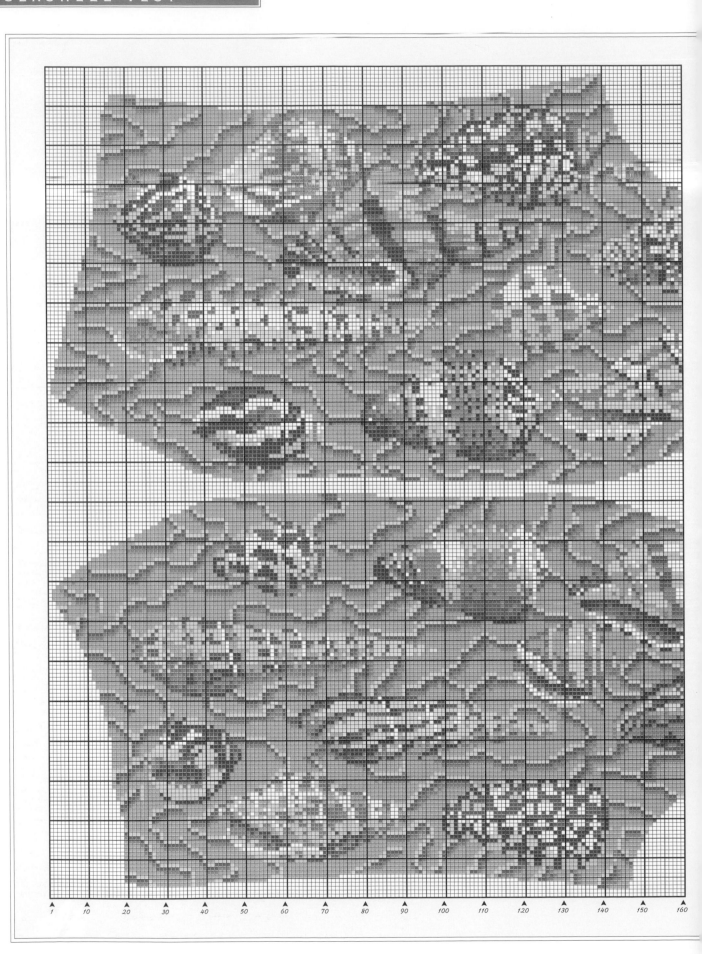

1   10   20   30   40   50   60   70   80   90   100   110   120   130   140   150   160

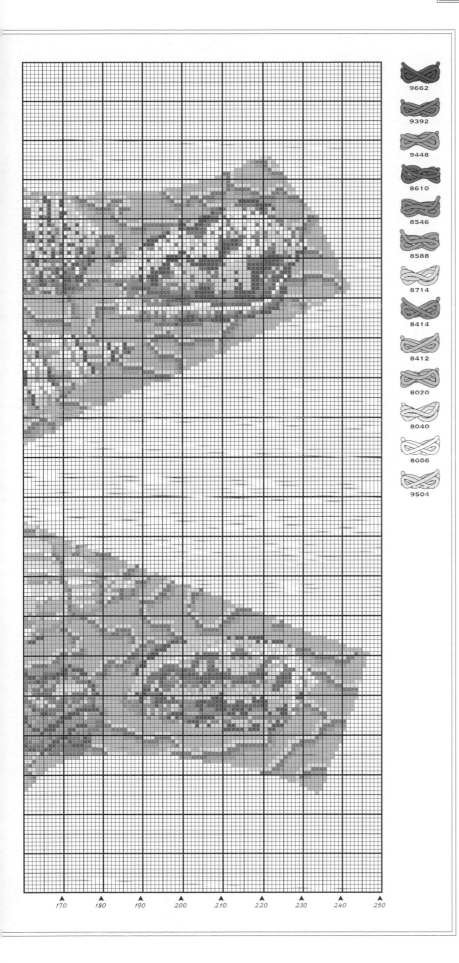

	9662
	9392
	9448
	8610
	8546
	8588
	8714
	8414
	8412
	8020
	8040
	8006
	9504

If you decide to back and line the vest yourself, turn to the instructions on pages 139–40. A needlepoint vest is for wearing and, like all clothes, needs cleaning from time to time. Take it to a good dry cleaner. Do not try to clean it yourself: it may shrink or distort, and after so much work, that would be heartbreaking. Our advice on cleaning any piece of needlepoint is always to get it dry-cleaned (it's better to be safe than sorry).

CANVAS: 10-gauge

STITCH: Half-cross or continental

DESIGN AREA: Top of neck to bottom of front points is 24 inches. Underarm to waist is 12 inches. Each front measures 10 inches across. When backed, it can be altered in size to fit up to a 40-inch bust.

YARN: Anchor tapisserie or Paternayan

Shade	Anchor	Paternayan	
Chocolate	9662	460	5 skeins
Cinnamon	9392	441	8 skeins
Nutmeg	9448	403	7 skeins
Periwinkle	8610	341	2 skeins
Lavender	8546	323	1 skein
Lilac	8588	313	2 skeins
Steel Gray	8714	D392	3 skeins
Raspberry	8414	D281	2 skeins
Raspberry	8412	924	2 skeins
Old Gold	8020	733	15 skeins
Maize	8040	753	3 skeins
Cream	8006	263	4 skeins
Bronze Flesh	9504	493	8 skeins

49

THE SEA

170 180 190 200 210 220 230 240 250

BIRD CATCHING A FISH

Neil McCallum's "Bird Catching a Fish" is based directly on a tile by William De Morgan, and he manages to catch all the fluid movement found in the original. He also faithfully reproduces the fresh, clean colors of De Morgan's ceramic tile, colors that De Morgan developed himself. There has been a resurgence of interest in De Morgan's work – Beth Russell of Designers' Forum, for example, has used some of his tile patterns for her own needlepoint kits. It is easy to see why. In addition to being a talented man with a distinctive signature, he was an interesting one. We remember him as an artist-potter, but he was better known to contemporaries as the author of a series of novels, all written between the ages of 67 and 78 – a sort of Mary Wesley of his day. Looking at his ceramics now, we can recognize in his approach a bridge between the mid-Victorian and the Pre-Raphaelite world of William Morris. As a potter, De Morgan is remembered best for his Persian styles, fabulous beasts (sometimes rather sinister combinations of animals), sailing ships, and exotic floral designs. The floral designs are usually set against complex patterns of twining, twisting vegetation, and here is probably the closest link with the textiles of William Morris. He was fascinated by all things scientific and was continually experimenting with ceramic technique. His colors became more vivid as he grew older, with the soft, glazed Persian colors of the early period at Chelsea giving way to luster and iridescence in the late 1880's.

The tile that Neil McCallum has chosen is from De Morgan's Persian period and is one of the most successful of his designs in terms of composition and line. The bird is also one of the more attractive of his fantastical creations – a combination of heron, stork, and peacock, by the look of it. Lewis Carroll was inspired to write *The Hunting of the Snark* by De Morgan tiles in his room at Oxford. The Jabberwock has its equivalent in De Morgan's dragons. The colors in the tile, dating from the early 1870's, used what he termed his Persian colors – a unique palette he developed consisting mainly of blue, turquoise, green, and clear red. To capture the detail of the design and, more importantly, to capture the clean sweep of De Morgan's lines, Neil McCallum chose a 14-gauge canvas. Often a simple design requires a clear outline, and the 14-gauge canvas is an integral part of this design's success. We should not forget that this picture was painted onto a tile. It is Neil's ability to elaborate and alter that enabled him to adapt the design just enough to translate it into needlework without jeopardizing the integrity of the original.

By the turn of the century, taste and fashion were moving in a different direction. The influence of Japanese simplicity, a primitive, rough quality to form and surface, and natural color were themes that interested artist-potters. "All my life I have been trying to make beautiful things and now that I can make them nobody wants them," said De Morgan sadly toward the end of his life. A similar fate befell William Morris and the whole of the Arts and Crafts movement. The seismic upheavals of modernism and the advent of the 20th century swept them aside. Within a matter of years, their work looked dated and quaintly irrelevant. It was light years away from Expressionist painting, the architectural theories of Le Corbusier, or the pottery of Bernard Leach. Only now that the tide of this turbulent storm-sea is receding with an exhausted, querulous clamor can we glimpse again the quieter achievements of these late-Victorian artists. Their aims were more modest, but their achievements were real. Looking now at De Morgan's work for what it is, not for what it represented, we see the expression of a confident draftsman with a pure, clear sense of color, an imaginative mind, and an idiosyncratic style.

NEIL McCALLUM'S RENDERING OF A
WILLIAM DE MORGAN TILE DESIGN – AN EXPERT
ADAPTATION IN EVERY RESPECT.

De Morgan's tiles still excite us today. It is not only their fantastic animal creations that make them unique, it is his bold, dramatic sense of design, which fills the available surface with rhythmic patterns. The purity of his colors – blues, turquoise, and greens, in particular – add to this sense of authority. He was greatly influenced by Persian Isnik tiles of the 15th and 16th centuries, with their fluent swirls and exotic curves. His tiles are an excellent design source because many of them are complete pictures in themselves. I particularly like some of his ships. The Victoria and Albert Museum in London has published a selection of his tile designs, and J. Catleugh's *William De Morgan (1839–1917) Tilemaker* was published in 1983. De Morgan designed the tile panels for the Czar Alexander III's yacht, *Livadia,* and he filled the gaps in Lord Leighton's Arabian Hall at his Kensington house with copies of the genuine Isnik tiles.

CANVAS: 14-gauge

STITCH: Half-cross or continental

DESIGN AREA: 15 × 15 inches

YARN: Appleton tapestry yarn or Paternayan

Shade	Appleton	Paternayan	
Kingfisher	481	584	4 skeins
Kingfisher	484	591	2 skeins
Kingfisher	487	581	3 skeins
Signal Green	437	681	1 skein
Charcoal	998	221	2 skeins
Pastel Cream	882	263	9 skeins
Autumn Yellow	478	721	1 skein
Royal Blue	824	540	2 skeins
Autumn Yellow	475	723	2 skeins
Honeysuckle Yellow	693	734	1 skein
Bright Peacock Blue	831	D522	2 skeins
Bright Peacock Blue	833	661	1 skein
Bright Peacock Blue	835	660	1 skein
Sea Green	403	611	2 skeins
Sea Green	401	613	2 skeins
Sea Green	407	660	3 skeins
Cornflower	462	544	6 skeins

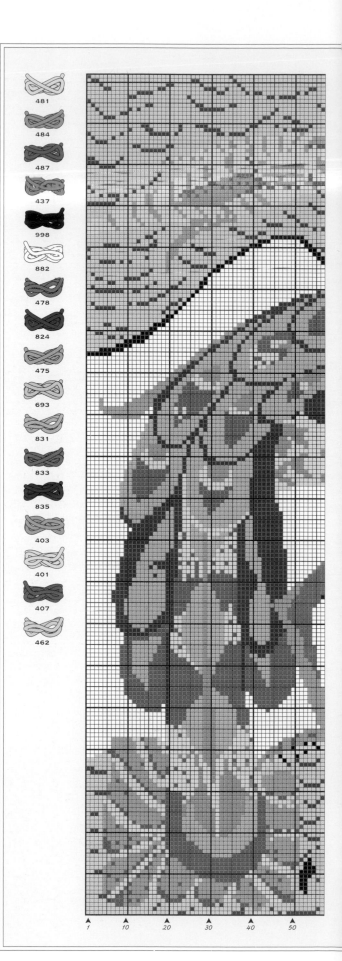

60 70 80 90 100 110 120 130 140 150 160 170 180 190 200 206

LINER

It is refreshing to be ending this chapter with Mike Wade's "Liner." It is a completely different subject and Mike's first needlepoint for us. Mike is a graphic designer by trade, and he has been designing our catalogs and advertisements for many years. Although he has no formal textile training, we decided it would be fun if Mike created a design for us, and the highly successful "Liner" is the result. Mike combines his skill in graphic perspective with his love of the sea, and his next two projects will also feature oceanic subjects.

Mike's design background is evident in the posterlike quality of this color-block composition. I always associate cruises with British ocean liners of the interwar years, and that image is the image of the poster. Mike captures this in limpid reflections and smoke trailing from funnels; full moons, blue lagoons, white tuxedos, martinis – a Hollywood world of escape. We have photographed it as a picture because that seemed the most obvious format, but it could make a stylish long pillow for a high-backed chair.

As a company, we have always encouraged designers unfamiliar with needlework to have a try. I learned last year that the architect Vanbrugh's first building was Castle Howard. Until then, his design experience was limited to stage sets. An extreme example, perhaps, of the inspired amateurism of that age, but something of this spirit needs to be recaptured. Our best designers like to work in a variety of materials. This is because they have a lot to say, and different jobs require different tools. Look at Kaffe Fassett, for example – a knitter, stitcher, and painter who makes rag rugs and designs complex fabric and wallpaper patterns. He has a sound technical understanding of how to work in all these disciplines and will suggest modifications to machinery or production processes to achieve the result he is look-

ing for. I am delighted that Peter Blake, the artist, should be designing for us and that we have a pillow in this book by Caroline Charles, the fashion designer. The more involvement from outside, the more experimentation, and the more cross-fertilization of ideas that we can bring to the world of needlework, the better. Let serendipity thrive.

Many of these new ideas prove to be uncommercial, but you can never tell which ones will catch on until you have tried them. Kaffe Fassett's "Cabbage" and "Cauliflower" were wonderful designs, but we thought they would probably be of limited appeal. They were our best-selling designs for more than two years. That sort of unexpected success gives everyone a boost and encourages us to believe that the scope of needlework design can be widened.

As needlework in general declined in Britain after World War II, the commercial industry narrowed its design focus to what seemed safe. That is the familiar path of a declining trade starved of cash and sympathy. Fear and disillusion then feed on themselves. There was less to stitch, so there were fewer stitchers. With fewer stitchers, there was even greater caution when producing new design because the leeway for error kept diminishing. It takes a brand-new approach to break out of this sort of cycle. The needlework trade got it in the late 1970's with the arrival of Kaffe Fassett. His input has led to the total transformation we see today. He made needlework an interesting subject to work in again, and as more stitchers were attracted, so were more designers. When we started our business in 1978, the only other "design-based" company was Glorafilia. At that time there were probably fewer than 100 kits to stitch in Britain. On my last visit to Liberty's needlecraft department, I stopped counting after 800. Times have changed, and a large measure of credit for this should go to Kaffe.

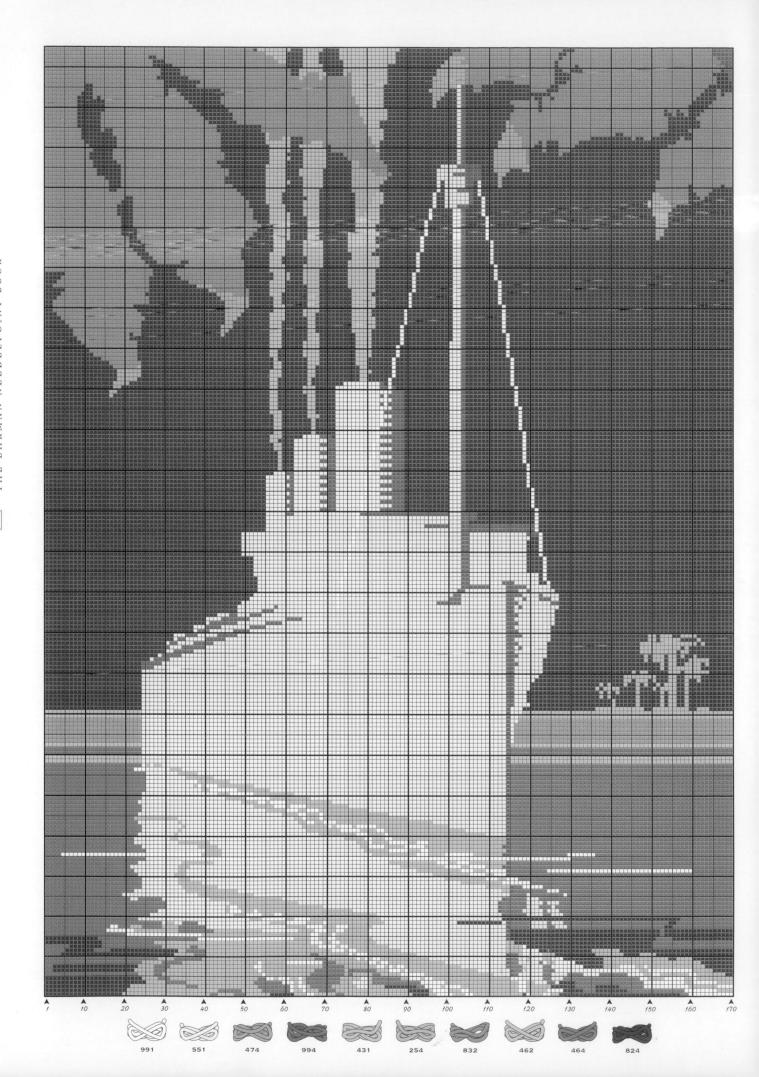

1   10   20   30   40   50   60   70   80   90   100   110   120   130   140   150   160   170

991   551   474   994   431   254   832   462   464   824

When we started our business, the majority of kits around were for pictures. On the whole, they were pretty awful: horses in the park, clowns with tears running down their cheeks, and a host of Last Suppers. I'm delighted to say that there are fewer of those around today. Needlepoint kits have gradually shifted in emphasis from stitched pictures to pillow covers, rugs, and chair cushions. Rex, the German shepherd, and semi-clad flamenco dancers may be in retreat, but a gap has been left for more "tasteful" pictures. There was never anything wrong with the idea of needlepoint pictures per se; it was just the subjects chosen and their crude coloring. Mike's "Liner" is certainly something new. A number of Jill Gordon's recent pillow designs would work equally well as pictures, especially her landscapes, and I suspect we may see a revival of stitched pictures. They are, after all, only smaller-scale wall hangings.

CANVAS: 12-gauge

STITCH: Half-cross or continental

DESIGN AREA: 20 × 14½ inches

YARN: Appleton tapestry yarn or Paternayan

Shade	Appleton	Paternayan	
Royal Blue	824	540	17 skeins
Cornflower	464	542	5 skeins
Cornflower	462	544	3 skeins
Bright Peacock Blue	832	662	5 skeins
Grass Green	254	692	1 skein
Autumn Yellow	474	725	1 skein
Rust	994	852	3 skeins
Signal Green	431	687	2 skeins
Bright Yellow	551	773	9 skeins
White	991	261	2 skeins

Chapter Three

~

NEW FLORALS

"There is no climate, no place, and scarcely an hour, in which nature does not exhibit color which no mortal effort can imitate or approach. For all our artificial pigments are, even when seen under the same circumstances, dead and lightless beside her living colour; nature exhibits her hues under an intensity of sunlight which trebles their brilliancy."

JOHN RUSKIN, *MODERN PAINTERS*, 1843

POSY OF FLOWERS

Elian McCready's flowers glow with a burnished radiance that lifts the spirits. This chapter is largely devoted to them, and it celebrates her joyous use of high color. These flowers are usually on a large scale, leaping out of the picture at you, and they transmit Elian's sheer delight in her subject.

Color is about stirring the emotions. When Chardin saw a fruit, the visual experience filled him with such enjoyment that it invested eye and hand with the capacity to paint as he did. When the Dutch painter Pieter de Hooch painted the roof of a house, he conveyed his own delight in the marvel of light, the wealth of colors, and the tones he saw.

BOLD SCALE AND BOLD COLOR TYPIFY THE WORK OF ELIAN MCCREADY (PICTURED OPPOSITE). HAVING WORKED FOR A NUMBER OF YEARS WITH KAFFE FASSETT, SHE NOW CONCENTRATES EXCLUSIVELY ON HER OWN DESIGNS.

The artist has to be moved for the beholder to be, and Elian clearly is. Lecturing on color in 1802, Henri Fuseli compared the eye's appreciation of color to the ear's appreciation of music: "Stern and deep-toned tints rouse, determine, invigorate the eye, as warlike sound or a deep bass the

ear; and bland, rosy, gray or vernal tints, smooth, calm or melt like a sweet melody." A little contrived, perhaps, but the analogy with music is often made by painters. David Hockney speaks of tone being like pitch in music, and the combinations of tones to create a general color effect can be compared to the combination of notes to create a single chord. After so much talk of painting with yarn, it is rather nice to imagine composing with yarn for a change.

Elian, like Kaffe Fassett and Jill Gordon, builds her compositions gradually, stitching her way forward. Colors are blended to build shaded pattern, and pyramids of color gradually emerge by a progressive heightening of color

intensity. It is a process that requires constant refinements, changes of direction, and experiments along the way.

Elian's method of stitching is tactile and immediate, and this requires a knowledge of and feel for her ingredients – colored yarns. It is the way she blends and mixes them at each stage that determines the eventual outcome. That is why she can produce such highly colored designs that manage to be subtle at the same time. The colors build gradually. However bright her work, it is never garish because color is not thrown down in primary blocks. By constantly mixing her shades, Elian "paints" or "composes" her creations. Strictly speaking, what she does not do is "design" them.

Design implies a preconceived blueprint that is then executed, as in designing a car or an alarm clock. Designers
often talk of "resolving a problem" or of "design solutions."
Elian's method is far more artistic, in the sense that an
artist lets the work, to a certain extent, evolve. She starts
with a general idea of what she wants to achieve and draws
a rough outline onto the canvas. The color, with all that
implies – shadow, perspective, depth – follows, and that
determines the true character of her work.

For many years Elian worked with Kaffe Fassett, and for
those of you who remember his "Flower Trellis" rug, the
bold composition of these flowers will have a familiar look.
Her flowers are always powerful. The scale of them in this
design would, I think, allow for a border if you wanted to
create a larger pillow. Maybe a geometric pattern using the
same colors she has, or perhaps a more fluid repeat pattern.

CANVAS: 10-gauge

STITCH: Half-cross or continental

DESIGN AREA: 16 × 16 inches

YARN: Appleton tapestry yarn or Paternayan

Shade	Appleton	Paternayan	
White	991	261	3 skeins
Off-white	992	263	4 skeins
Medium Blue	156	532	2 skeins
Peacock Blue	643	602	2 skeins
Peacock Blue	642	D546	2 skeins
Gray Green	352	605	2 skeins
Dull Mauve	935	D115	2 skeins
Bright Rose Pink	941	934	3 skeins
Bright Rose Pink	943	932	2 skeins
Bright Rose Pink	944	904	3 skeins
Bright Rose Pink	946	903	2 skeins
Coral	862	854	2 skeins
Coral	864	832	2 skeins
Bright Mauve	451	323	2 skeins
Bright Mauve	453	302	2 skeins
Fuchsia	801	353	2 skeins
Fuchsia	805	350	2 skeins
Wine Red	716	910	3 skeins
Bright Rose Pink	948	901	3 skeins
Hyacinth	895	310	1 skein
Bright Yellow	551	773	2 skeins
Bright Yellow	554	771	2 skeins
Bright China Blue	741	564	1 skein

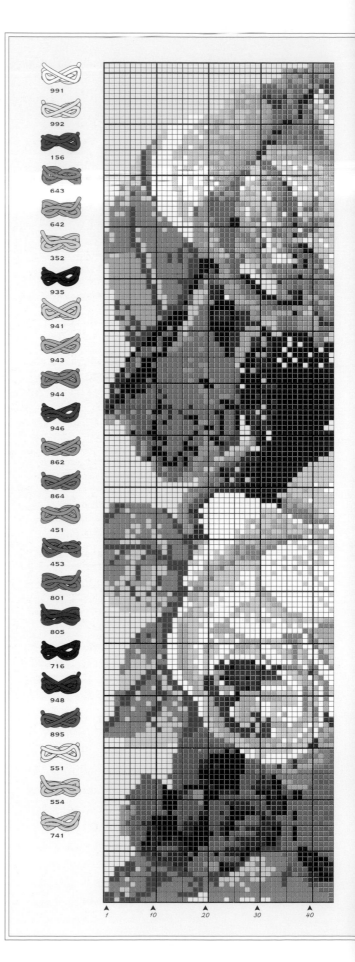

50 60 70 80 90 100 110 120 130 140 150 160 165

LILIES

As you can see from Zöe and Tim Hill's luxuriantly rich photograph on the following page, the "Lilies" and "Nasturtiums" work as a color group. They were designed by Elian McCready in the same year. The oranges and burnt sienna smolder against her azure blue skies. The blue backing of "Nasturtiums" in particular is the blue of intense cobalt – a saturated French blue reminiscent of the Mediterranean. These designs are shafts of sunlight that would cheer up any room.

"Lilies" makes a standard-size pillow, while "Nasturtiums," stitched on the same 10-gauge canvas, is larger, measuring 20 × 20 inches. The panel looks much larger, but it is actually 30 × 30 inches. It is the way it is stitched that adds to the impression of size. It is worked in random long stitch, which gives the surface its silky texture and feeling of depth. Unfortunately, this type of long stitch is only suitable for canvases that are destined for the wall. Pillows or cushions worked in this way would quickly fray and pull out of shape. Elian worked for many years with Kaffe Fassett, and random long stitch was a method he adapted and developed for his commissioned large hangings. It is quicker to work and gives a more fluid, "painterly" feel to the design. The kit comes with a preprinted color canvas, so you don't have to work from a chart. Elian has now completed a series of four floral hangings, this being the last. The first, "Pansies," has proved to be the most popular so far, but I would not be surprised if "Nasturtiums" ran a close second. It is certainly one of her best.

NASTURTIUMS

Elian was originally a painter, and it shows. She has a painter's eye for color shading, like Jill Gordon and Kaffe Fassett, and any similarities that are still visible in their approach to needlework design are not coincidental. They have all worked together at one time or another. In the mid-1970's Kaffe set up a cooperative workshop in Gloucestershire, England, with Lillian Delevoryas (Lillian now lives in America, but examples of her work can be found in our earlier catalogs). It was called the Weatherall workshop, and among those in residence were Jill Gordon and Sarah Windrum, both of whom are designers we work with regularly. When the workshop closed and Kaffe moved back to London, something of this spirit returned with him, and throughout the 1980's a fluc-tuating group of stitchers and designers gathered around him to help on his many projects. The most regular of these were Jill Gordon and Elian McCready, and a whole school of design, based around Kaffe, emerged. They have now both gone their separate ways, producing their own designs. Sadly, we have only one of Jill's, "Savonnerie," in this book, on page 123. She publishes her own book this year and, quite correctly, has reserved all her new work for it. It is a magnificent collection, and many of these new designs will be in our 1996 catalog. Elian also concentrates entirely on her own work these days, which gets better and better. Luckily, she did not have a book coming out this year! This trio of designs are among the best in the book, and I am delighted that we have the space to do them justice.

This is primarily an exercise in shading, but it was also the first design to use sky and a descending depth of color for the background. All of Elian's previous designs had simple colored backgrounds (where there was a background at all). The sky adds perspective and, with it, a new dimension to the whole design. Jill Gordon used descending tones of blue as a background for a fire screen of butterflies she stitched recently. It is very effective, drawing you into the picture. Here is a useful design tip, particularly for designs with a limited area of background. It immediately alters the character of the composition and gives it a lift.

CANVAS: 10-gauge

STITCH: Half-cross or continental

DESIGN AREA: 16 × 16 inches

YARN: Appleton tapestry yarn or Paternayan

Shade	Appleton	Paternayan	
Dull Rose Pink	148	900	1 skein
Brown Olive	312	D531	2 skeins
Dull Marine Blue	327	510	2 skeins
Gray Green	353	604	2 skeins
Cornflower	461	564	4 skeins
Autumn Yellow	474	725	2 skeins
Scarlet	504	950	3 skeins
Turquoise	527	D502	2 skeins
Bright Yellow	553	772	2 skeins
Bright Yellow	557	812	2 skeins
Sky Blue	564	584	2 skeins
Mauve	606	310	1 skein
Royal Blue	822	542	3 skeins
Bright Peacock Blue	832	662	2 skeins
Coral	864	832	6 skeins
Pastel Lilac	885	313	1 skein
White	991	261	2 skeins
Rust	994	852	6 skeins
Lemon	996	673	2 skeins
Lime	997	672	1 skein
Charcoal	998	221	1 skein

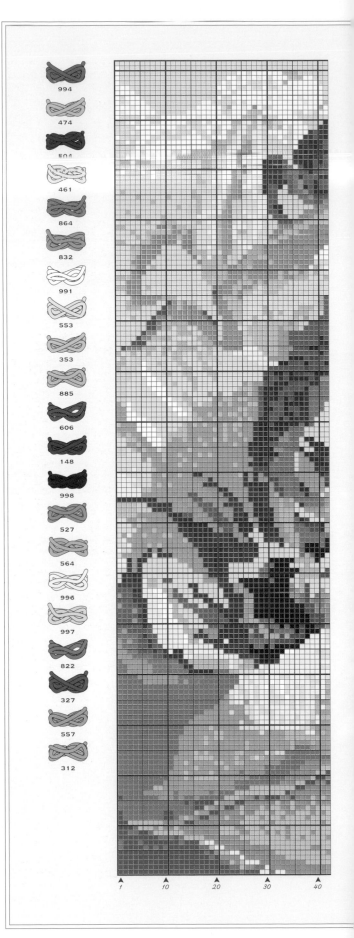

50 60 70 80 90 100 110 120 130 140 150 160 166

Elian combines really strong colors to glorious effect. Her innate sense of color balance never lets her down, even when she is testing the upper limits of the chromatic Richter scale.

CANVAS: 10-gauge

STITCH: Half-cross or continental

DESIGN AREA: 20 × 20 inches

YARN: Paternayan

Shade	Paternayan	
Plum	320	2 skeins
Damson	900	3 skeins
Plum	321	2 skeins
Cherry Red	840	4 skeins
Burnt Sienna	852	5 skeins
Cherry Red	842	4 skeins
Orange	832	3 skeins
Yellow	812	4 skeins
Yellow	815	3 skeins
Butterscotch	702	2 skeins
Bright Yellow	712	2 skeins
Pale Yellow	727	2 skeins
Plum	322	1 skein
Plum	324	1 skein
Cobalt Blue	541	4 skeins
Bright Lime	671	2 skeins
Pine Green	531	1 skein
Peacock Green	520	2 skeins
Pine Green	532	2 skeins
Peacock Green	521	4 skeins
Peacock Green	522	5 skeins

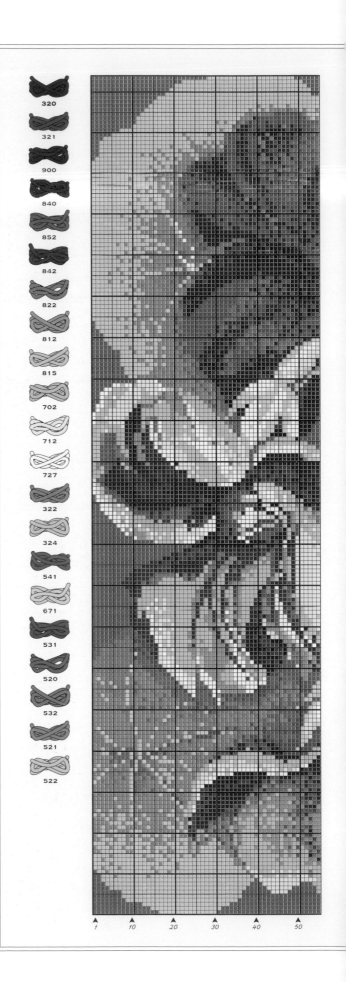

60　70　80　90　100　110　120　130　140　150　160　170　180　190　200　210

GREEN NOSEGAY

Kaffe Fassett's first voyages to the outer limits of neon color were greeted with horror by many. Such color use seemed a betrayal of all the efforts to educate popular taste in an appreciation of soft, pastel shades. It was like Bob Dylan going electric! But others loved it, and for the past three or four years, Kaffe has been experimenting, intermittently, with luminous shock contrasts. As usual, he was simply moving ahead of the times. You only have to look at modern furnishing fabrics or interior design magazines to see how others have caught up. As we have become more used to seeing dramatic hues around us, the level of complaint we receive about Kaffe's "unnatural use of color" has diminished correspondingly.

Natural color is something of a myth, at least in painting. What any artist does with color is personal and is, to some extent, unnatural. A natural use of color is extremely rare in the history of art and, as the experiments of Turner and the Impressionists showed, extremely difficult to determine. When we see the real colors in nature, we are apt to complain about their unreality. Kaffe Fassett is always keen to point out that colors in nature are often far stronger than we imagine. Look at some flowers close up, and you will find them astonishingly bright. In nature, however, they are toned down by the far larger areas of duller colors that surround them.

The overall design of Kaffe's "Green Nosegay" is so electric because of the decorative framework Kaffe chooses for the pattern. He has taken strong natural colors for the flowers and surrounded them with an unnatural continuation of the same, and that is why they look so unusual. His confidence with really bright color is unique, and I wanted to feature this design for that reason. The original "Ribbon Nosegay" was worked on a plum-colored background, which somehow flattened the design. Kaffe was unhappy with it and decided on a new approach. By placing it on this neon grass green, the whole thing comes to life and suddenly all the bright colors look good together.

This is one of the rare Kaffe Fassett designs that is stitched on 12-gauge canvas to capture the detail. The inspiration for this pillow was one of Kaffe's own vests, stitched in petitpoint, with a luscious combination of fruits and flowers. After the large dimensions of Elian McCready's "Lilies" and "Nasturtiums," it is nice to have a pillow stitched on a smaller scale.

DIZZY COLORS FROM THE WORLD'S MOST
ADVENTUROUS STITCHER. KAFFE FASSETT IS ALWAYS MOVING ON.
BY THE TIME PEOPLE HAVE BECOME USED TO ONE STYLE,
HE IS ALREADY WORKING ON THE NEXT.

1 10 20 30 40 50 60 70 80 90 100 110 120 130 140

If the border or green background are not to your taste, you could use the central group of flowers in a number of other ways. I think the combination of the bright green with the high colors of the flowers is the essence of this design, but I can see that the finished product might be too strong for some people's furnishings. If that is so, don't just pass this design by. Set the flowers against a black or French blue background (like Elian McCready's "Nasturtiums" background) for a totally different effect. Stitched in this way, the design would make a lively smaller pillow with the outer leaves and petals stretching to the edge of the canvas. Bordered with decorative braid or cord, the pillow would measure roughly 12 to 13 inches square, or it could be set in a wider fabric border.

CANVAS: 12-gauge

STITCH: Half-cross or continental

DESIGN AREA: 16 × 16 inches

YARN: Paternayan

Shade	Paternayan	
Bright Lime	670	8 skeins
Plum	320	1 skein
Pale Violet	340	1 skein
Bright Lavender	332	2 skeins
Pink	946	1 skein
Pink	943	1 skein
Scarlet	972	2 skeins
Damson	901	2 skeins
Strawberry	950	1 skein
Cherry Red	843	1 skein
Ginger Brown	883	1 skein
Jade Green	655	1 skein
Bright Lime	671	1 skein
Bright Yellow	712	1 skein
Jade Green	653	2 skeins
Leaf Green	693	1 skein
Leaf Green	692	2 skeins
Hunter Green	610	5 skeins
Pink	944	1 skein

FOXGLOVES AND DELPHINIUMS

After the wild and colorful intoxication of the past 16 pages, Ann Blockley's pair of hangings offers a breather.

Ingres's advice to Degas to "draw lines, many lines, from memory or nature; it is by this that you will become a good artist" applies particularly to botanical drawing. It is endless observation, not an adherence to mathematical principles, that lies at the heart of successful flower painting. Ann Blockley is a watercolorist, and her two panels capture the washed feel of watercolor. This is especially true of the abstract backgrounds. The foxgloves and delphiniums are drawn with a practiced eye, and although she presented the artwork on graph paper, with each stitched square marked out, she managed to retain the dynamic of her original watercolor paintings. In some ways, they remind me of Japanese screen panels or Chinese scroll paintings, with their long, thin dimensions and focus on individual flowers.

In the East the tradition of painting flowers from natural observation had religious origins. In China, Buddhist art was a powerful stimulus to flower painting. The demand for flower-filled skies in paradise scenes and for flower borders on religious banners and wall paintings prompted painters to study floral form in detail. In the case of Japan, we think of traditional folding screens decorated with plants, bamboo, or flowers. Flower studies in the West had medicinal, rather than religious, origins. Italian and German herbal books of the 14th century used material rediscovered in the first-century volumes of the Greek medical expert Dioscorides. They are remarkably similar to the studies of fruits and flowers found in the pattern books of the early 15th-century tapestry weavers. This Western tradition of natural study reached its apotheosis in the late 15th century with Albrecht Dürer's hyperrealistic depictions of animals, flowers, and plant life.

The study of individual flowers is common to all parts of the world. People have always had an irrepressible imperative to record the world around them, but they have studied flowers for another reason: a delight in form and color for their own sake. Flowers are one of the wonders of the world, and we are driven to paint, stitch, and photograph them. We simply can't help it – they are irresistible, and every generation of artists tries to capture them at some stage.

I first saw Ann's work in the British magazine *Country Living*. It showed a pair of her paintings, watercolors of geese and pheasants, which I thought would make good needlepoint designs. She was interested in the idea and over the next two or three years went on to produce a series of five kits, all based on farmyard animals or animals native to Gloucestershire, England, where she lives. Her "Geese" were particularly popular. But five was enough, and she wanted a change. The idea of these two panels was entirely her own, and she regards them as more truly her own work. I think they have worked out very successfully and add something fresh and different to our collection. Her choice of foxgloves and delphiniums and their unembellished presentation (no stylized borders or motifs) give these designs a natural "garden" feel.

The background drifts of color involve numerous color changes. The odd misplaced stitch, however, will make no difference in the finished piece. Shading of this subtlety is achieved by blending tones almost stitch by stitch, and when working the printed canvas from one of our kits, it is inevitable that one or two stitches will be unclear. It doesn't matter. The nature of these designs implies a certain irregularity, and it is the irregularity of needlework that is part of its charm. You are not stitching straight lines here, and the message from all our designers is to relax and enjoy it.

HERE WE FIND NEEDLEWORK THAT COULD ALMOST BE WATERCOLOR. THE DISTEMPERED WASH OF THE ABSTRACT BACKGROUNDS GIVES A UNIQUE FEEL TO ANN BLOCKLEY'S TWO PANELS.

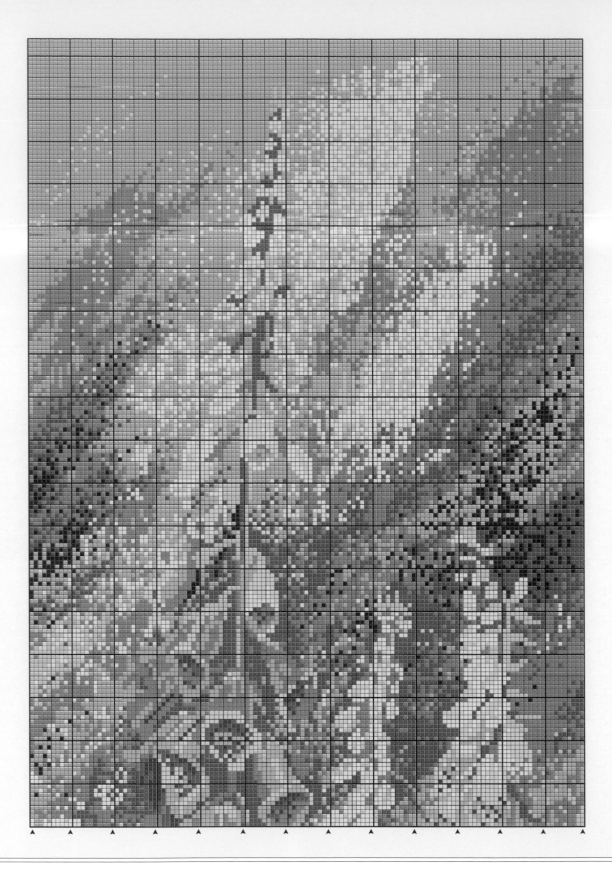

CANVAS: 10-gauge

STITCH: Half-cross or continental

DESIGN AREA: 37 × 13 inches

YARN: Anchor tapisserie or Paternayan

Shade	Anchor	Paternayan	
Autumn Gold	8054	754	3 skeins
Laurel	9002	663	6 skeins
Forest Green	9020	602	11 skeins
Forest Green	9022	600	8 skeins
Sea Green	8904	510	2 skeins

Shade	Anchor	Paternayan		Shade	Anchor	Paternayan	
Peacock Green	8924	521	3 skeins	Raspberry	8412	901	5 skeins
Sea Green	8894	203	5 skeins	Raspberry	8414	901	4 skeins
Sea Green	8898	514	9 skeins	Raspberry	8418	912	2 skeins
Lavender	8542	323	4 skeins	Damson	8508	922	3 skeins

CANVAS: 10-gauge

STITCH: Half-cross or continental

DESIGN AREA: 37 × 13 inches

YARN: Anchor tapisserie or Paternayan

Shade	Anchor	Paternayan	
Spruce Green	9080	600	5 skeins
Spruce Green	9078	601	5 skeins
Spruce Green	9076	602	8 skeins
Sea Green	8896	514	10 skeins
Periwinkle	8610	341	2 skeins

9080

9078

9076

8896

8610

8608

8604

8714

9388

9214

9256

8006

8898

81

N E W   F L O R A L S

Shade	Anchor	Paternayan		Shade	Anchor	Paternayan	
Periwinkle	8608	342	3 skeins	Moss Green	9214	694	3 skeins
Periwinkle	8604	343	2 skeins	Sage Green	9256	644	4 skeins
Steel Gray	8714	213	3 skeins	Cream	8006	263	3 skeins
Cinnamon	9388	442	5 skeins	Sea Green	8898	533	2 skeins

FRUIT DROPS

We end the chapter as we started it – with a fiery blaze of Elian McCready color. This is not a floral design, but it seemed appropriate for this chapter. Fruits and flowers go well together. We have only two designs based on fruit in the whole book, this one and Neil McCallum's "Chalice of Fruit" in the last chapter. This is surprising, because for two or three years our catalog was like a produce market. Elian was very much part of that trend. She was working with Kaffe Fassett at the time, and he was primarily responsible for the fructification of our range. There is no doubt that she learned a lot from his fruit-stitching technique. Her "Fruit Drops" have the same lustrous quality that Kaffe gets into his pears, apples, plums, and lemons. In his memorable "Apple and Cabbage" carpet, Kaffe grouped fruits and vegetables in a generous profusion, but his pillow-cover kits tended to be single studies: cherries, melons, plums. Their bold scale was part of their success. Here Elian stitches her fruits in a similar way, mixing yarns to paint highlights, but uses them as elements grouped within an overall composition. On this smaller scale she still manages to evoke a skillful impression of their surface texture.

The color balance is similar to that in her earlier group. An effulgent cocktail of glimmering embers, with brighter sparks of pink, yellow, and crimson, shines from a blue backdrop – in this case, a darker blue. The speckled background adds a new element – a touch of merriment – while balancing the design. Here is another familiar Kaffe Fassett/Elian McCready touch. I remember a spectacular chair Kaffe stitched for the couture designer Sonia Rykiel, with fruits and flowers on a black background sprayed with white dots. Speckling lifts the design and can be a useful device for backgrounds that need a bit of spicing up.

The art historian and poet Herbert Read divided the use of color in painting into three general categories: the "heraldic," the "harmonic," and the "pure." The "heraldic" was the most primitive and died out in the Middle Ages. Color was used for symbolic significance and was static, so that the robe of the Virgin always had to be blue, her cloak red, and so on. In the next stage, the "harmonic," tonal values and relative intensity involved regulating colors to conform to a restricted scale. A dominant tone was selected, and all other colors were scaled up or down to a restricted distance from this scale. The general practice from the 16th to the 18th century was to work from a scaled palette, your colors neatly laid out within a narrow range. A perfect example of the harmonic use of color would be the work of the Dutch painter Van Goyen. In quite separate ways, both Turner and Constable rebelled against this tradition and formed a bridge to the later world of "pure" color, in which color is used for its own sake – Matisse being the most obvious example this century. Colors are taken in their purest intensity, and pattern is built up in contrasts of relative intensity. Because the main purpose is decorative, questions of verisimilitude are secondary. Color is reduced to its most direct, sensuous appeal. Looked at in this way, color has always been in the eye of the beholder, or more exactly in the imagination of the beholder, and the brighter colors we see in this chapter justify the title "New Florals." They are clearly colored in what Herbert Read would term the "pure" manner, and they appeal on a sensuous and decorative level.

This chapter has been about shading, stitching graded dots of color to build an image. There are many other needlework techniques for designing flowers. In the first chapter we have the "Berlin Roses." These were adapted from Berlin Woolwork charts, which built up petals and leaves with an almost photographic precision. They used a lot of colors and a fine gauge of canvas to achieve an equally subtle result. But the design technique was quite different. It depended on contrasting shades of light with dark to define color blocks. It was a more graphic approach to color

FRUITS AND LEAVES FROM ELIAN ON A SMALLER SCALE THAN USUAL BUT WITH A FAMILIAR INTENSITY OF HIGH COLORS, SET THIS TIME ON A SPOTTED BACKGROUND.

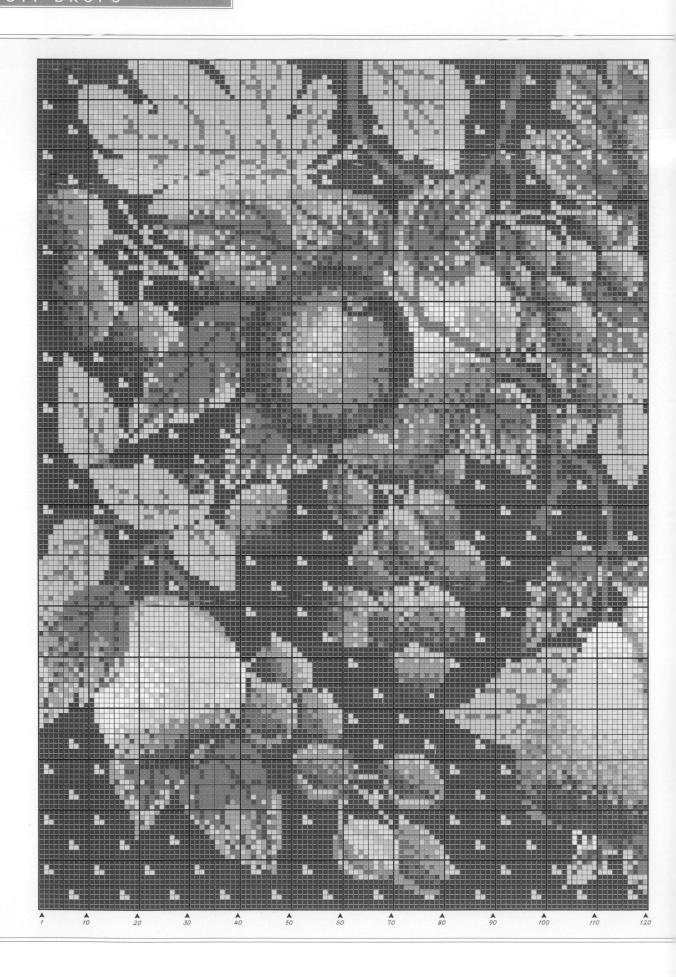

1   10   20   30   40   50   60   70   80   90   100   110   120

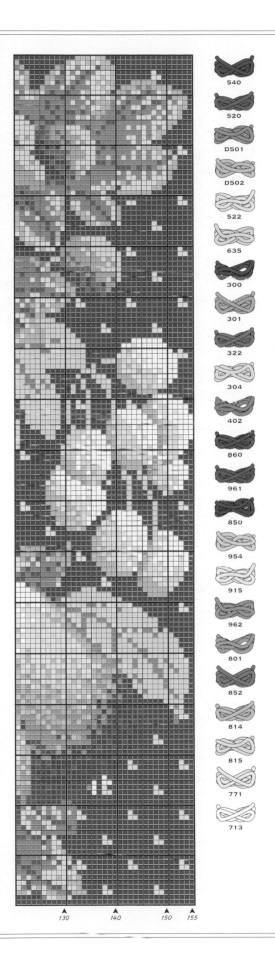

differentiation. The spring flowers in the "Alphabet Pillow," at the start of Chapter 5, are simplified down to two or three colors for each flower. No technique is "better" than any other; they can all be equally effective. What is true, however, is that the technique we have looked at in this chapter is unique. Kaffe Fassett, Elian McCready, and Jill Gordon have developed a needlework technique of painting with yarn that is entirely their own.

Drenched in the golden light of evening, Elian's fruits are illuminated against the darkening sky. "Blazing in Gold and quenching in Purple" is how the poet Emily Dickinson once described a sunset, and a similar drama is being enacted here on Elian's canvas.

CANVAS: 10-gauge

STITCH: Half-cross or continental

DESIGN AREA: 16½ × 15½ inches

YARN: Paternayan

Shade	Paternayan	
Cobalt Blue	540	8 skeins
Peacock Green	520	2 skeins
Turquoise	D501	3 skeins
Turquoise	D502	2 skeins
Peacock Green	522	2 skeins
Pale Spring Green	635	3 skeins
Purple	300	1 skein
Purple	301	2 skeins
Plum	322	2 skeins
Purple	304	1 skein
Brown	402	1 skein
Rust	860	1 skein
Bright Pink	961	1 skein
Burnt Sienna	850	1 skein
Strawberry	954	1 skein
Pale Pink	915	1 skein
Bright Pink	962	1 skein
Marigold	801	1 skein
Burnt Sienna	852	1 skein
Yellow	814	1 skein
Yellow	815	1 skein
Bright Yellow	771	2 skeins
Bright Yellow	713	1 skein

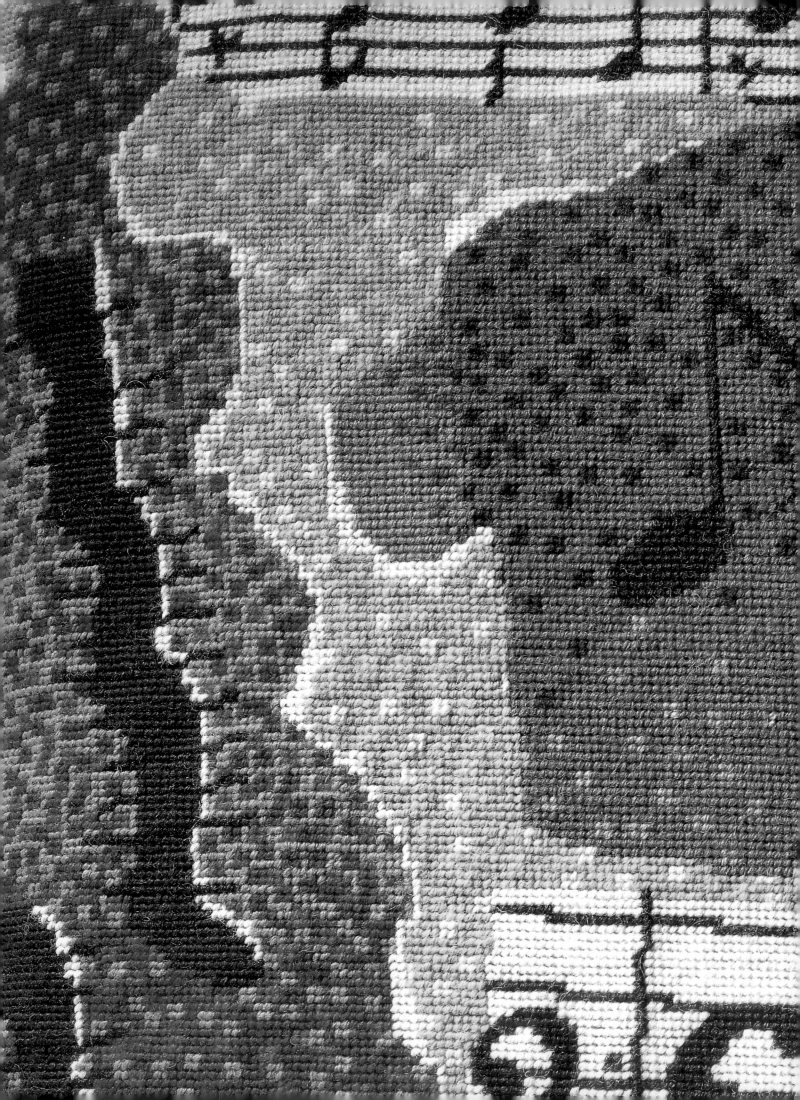

Chapter Four

~

A LIGHTER TOUCH

"Humor is the great thing, the saving thing after all. The minute it crops up, all our hardnesses yield, all our irritations and resentments flit away, and a sunny spirit takes their place."

MARK TWAIN, FROM HIS ESSAY
WHAT PAUL BOURGET THINKS OF US, 1895

CROWN

The more demanding life becomes, the more important it is to maintain a sense of proportion and a sense of humor. All our designers have a good sense of humor, thank God, and none take themselves too seriously. A sense of the ridiculous often goes hand in hand with an enjoyment of the unexpected. In design terms this means a quick eye for a visual joke, a lively, inquiring mind, and a healthy disdain for the obvious. This outlook is most commonly witnessed today in advertising. Advertising often relies for its impact on taking a familiar situation and turning it upside down. It was difficult to think of a title for this chapter. All the designs have a touch of levity. The element of humor, for want of a better word, lies simply in the fact that they make you smile. The

designs are graphic and bold and focus on their subject matter. They have a lighter touch, a metaphorical spring in their step, and a sense of fun. Their common denominator is a *joie de vivre*. What better design to kick off with than Caroline Charles's "Crown"?

Contact was made with Caroline Charles via a mutual friend. I was a little surprised and quite delighted to hear that one of Britain's top fashion designers was interested in designing a needlepoint kit with us. In fact, she designed two, the "Crown" and the "Last Stitch," of which the "Crown," I think, is the more successful. Her design department was very thorough, experimenting with a number of different combinations until they were satisfied. The design itself is punchy and stylish (as you would expect), but

the colors are beautifully judged, with considerable thought going into their selection. The result is a pillow that is fun without being gimmicky, and it will appeal to a whole new group of stitchers.

I am writing this on the day that Caroline is opening a new store in Bond Street, London. What she describes as her fit, small business is going through a phase of fairly dramatic expansion. Along with her other shop in Beauchamp Place, London, her burgeoning empire encompasses wholesaling and retailing, with new ranges of bedding, shoes, sunglasses, and bags, as well as the clothes. Like Paul Smith (Britain's other most successful fashion designer), she is extending her lucrative Japanese licensing operation and is a consultant to the British company Marks and Spencer. The

CAROLINE CHARLES IS ONE OF BRITAIN'S LEADING FASHION DESIGNERS, AND HERE SHE TURNS HER HAND TO NEEDLEPOINT FOR THE FIRST TIME, WITH HUMOR, ENERGY, AND PANACHE, AS YOU WOULD EXPECT.

secret of her success is that she has a clear idea of where she is going and who her customers are. At a youthful-looking 50, she has a wealth of experience stretching back to the early sixties, when she worked for Mary Quant. Her first collection was put together in London in 1963.

Caroline has always had a connection with needlework. She started sewing at her convent school so that she could whip up dresses for important occasions. Before Mary Quant she worked for Michael Sherrard in Curzon Street, London, where she learned every sort of couture sewing technique. "It was 70 percent hand-sewing; even the seams inside the linings were oversewn by hand." Knowing this now, I am far less surprised that she should have wanted to design a needlepoint kit. She loves the idea of anything new and has an infectious enthusiasm for whatever she is doing. We have tried working with fashion designers before, but their designs did not succeed because they simply trans-ferred fabric pattern onto canvas. Caroline designs a needle-point as a needlepoint. She does not use needlework as a vehicle for extending a particular design style. Her work has a rigor and discipline that eschews such indulgence.

CANVAS: 12-gauge

STITCH: Half-cross or continental

DESIGN AREA: 18 × 18 inches

YARN: Appleton tapestry yarn or Paternayan

Shade	Appleton	Paternayan	
Dark Damson Pink	948	901	2 skeins
Scarlet	501	951	3 skeins
Bright Rose Pink	946	903	1 skein
Charcoal	998	221	6 skeins
Putty Grounding	988	465	7 skeins
Sky Blue	568	500	4 skeins
Purple	106	312	1 skein
Early English Green	545	691	3 skeins
Gray Green	358	600	2 skeins
Autumn Yellow	474	725	5 skeins
Heraldic Gold	842	734	5 skeins
Off White	992	263	1 skein

This pillow is hard to classify. It is more masculine than most of our designs, but with an element of camp, a bit of a joke but chic at the same time. Like so much that is stylish, it is ambivalent, and this gives it a wider potential audience. You could take the central section of the "Crown," put it on a 10-gauge canvas to make it a little larger, and stitch it as a cut-out, like Kaffe Fassett's "Lily-Pad Frog." You could stitch a number of "crowns" by themselves and experiment with different colored backgrounds. I also think the tasseled border is rather good and could be used effectively on other designs. Being designed in clearly separated sections, this is a good pattern for adapting and having fun with: a design-er's design to enjoy.

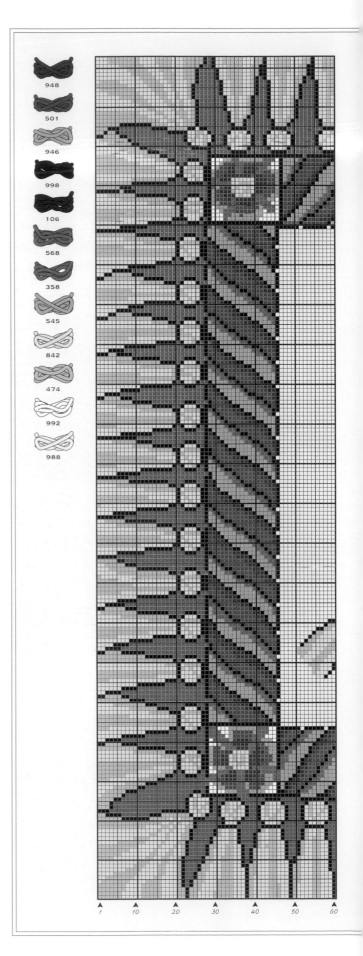

70   80   90   100   110   120   130   140   150   160   170   180   190   200   210   220

ALBION
AND
AMERICA

These two designs from Candace Bahouth are an interesting combination of the old and the new. There is the graphic, Pop art immediacy of the flag, but in both cases, it is a flag of historical reference, a flag you would associate with the folk art of either country. It is most appropriate that these two designs should have come from Candace – an American who has made her home in England – and they have all the style and charm we have come to associate with her needlework.

Most countries in the world take pride in their national flag but in varying degrees. In Europe, for example, the French have a far stronger attachment to their Tricolor than the Germans have to theirs. The historical reasons are obvious and, in any case, the present German flag was adopted only in 1949. The British, like the French, have a deep-rooted pride in their flag, but on the whole, it is an unobtrusive pride. These distinctions become marginal when compared with the pride that Americans take in their flag. When antiwar protesters burned their national flag in public in the 1960's, it was a more shocking act of defiance than it would have been in any European country. The United States is awash with Stars and Stripes from coast to coast. It would be almost impossible to spend a day anywhere in America without seeing at least one image of the flag. Flags don't fly just on public buildings. They fly in hundreds of thousands (possibly millions) on flagpoles erected in suburban lawns across the land. The bicentennial celebrations brought home what a new country America

THE UNION JACK, BLOWING IN THE BREEZE, IS STITCHED
BY CANDACE BAHOUTH, AN AMERICAN WHO HAS MADE HER
HOME IN THE HEART OF THE ENGLISH COUNTRYSIDE NEAR
GLASTONBURY IN SOMERSET.

still is, and the flag is a symbolic image of unity – the American way of life made tangible – for individuals from all over the world making a new life together. As a British citizen owes allegiance to the throne, so an American owes allegiance to the flag.

The Albion (an Old English word for Great Britian) flag presented the greater problem for Candace. You have to be careful with the Union Jack these days. It is a sad fact that it has been partially hijacked by the extreme Right and, used in the wrong way, can convey all the wrong sort of messages. A way around this was to return to a flag of historical reference, and if the pillows were to be designed as a pair, it was the obvious thing to do anyway. Candace's British flag is based on one she found on a cigarette card and has the same fresh, breezy invigoration as its American counterpart.

The term *Jack* was first used in the British navy to describe the Union flag that was, in the early 17th century, flown at the main masthead. It was an affectionate nickname meaning "small", an ironic reference to the flag's large size. By the late 17th century the term had stuck, and a vote in the Houses of Parliament in May 1660 refers to "standards, fflags and Jacke colours of the ffleets." In typically eccentric fashion, the United Kingdom is one of the few countries in the world that has no official national flag. The Union flag officially remains the sovereign's. It can, by common practice, be used by British subjects ashore, but the Merchant Shipping Act of 1894 expressly forbids its use afloat.

The flag itself is an amalgam of the national flags of England, Scotland, and Ireland. St. George became the patron saint of England in 1277, and his cross was first used as the emblem of England during the Welsh wars of Edward I. The origins of the Scottish flag go back further, as legend would have it, to 736 A.D., when Angus, Son of Fergus, King of the Picts, adopted St. Andrew as his patron saint. St. Andrew had been crucified on a diagonal cross in 69 A.D. The cross of St. George (red on a white ground) was joined by the white saltire (or diagonal) cross of St. Andrew on its blue ground in 1603, when James I united the thrones of England and Scotland. The flag of St. Patrick was added in 1801 with the incorporation of Ireland into the Union of Great Britain. The cross of St. Patrick, like that of St. George, is red on white but, like the cross of St. Andrew, goes from corner to corner. The Union Jack, by sacrificing most of the white background, combines the distinctive features of all three.

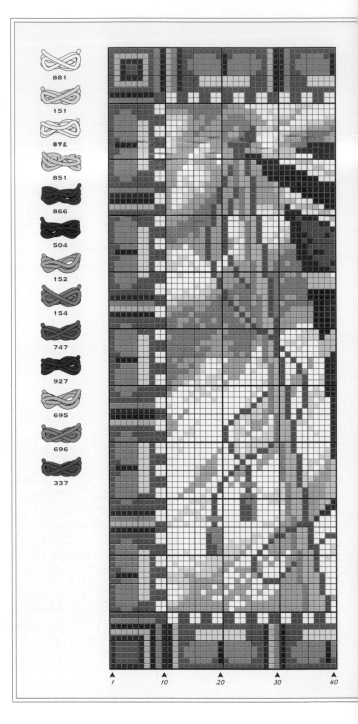

CANVAS: 10-gauge

STITCH: Half-cross or continental

DESIGN area: $15^{1}/_{2} \times 11$ inches

YARN: Appleton tapestry yarn or Paternayan

Shade	Appleton	Paternayan	
Pastel Cream	881	262	3 skeins
Medium Blue	151	203	2 skeins
Pastel Yellow	872	715	2 skeins
Custard Yellow	851	D541	2 skeins

Shade	Appleton	Paternayan	
Coral	866	850	2 skeins
Scarlet	504	950	2 skeins
Medium Blue	152	514	2 skeins
Medium Blue	154	534	2 skeins
Bright China Blue	747	500	2 skeins
Dull China Blue	927	510	2 skeins
Honeysuckle Yellow	695	732	1 skein
Honeysuckle Yellow	696	740	2 skeins
Drab Green	337	451	2 skeins

Flags are a splendid idea for needlepoint. We have started with the Union Jack and the Stars and Stripes as obvious choices, but combinations of flags would look equally good. There are books of flags published in which the flags are set out in series – naval, heraldic, regional. They would make excellent material for design. Most flags have fairly straight-forward blocks and so would be simple to stitch. In groups they are both elegant and graphic. Albion's border gets lost here, and it might be better to stitch out a little farther so that it becomes more visible when the pillow is backed.

Both Candace and I had the idea for the American flag at about the same time. I had seen a wonderful 19th century American fabric with the Stars and Stripes used as the main motif. Most versions of the American flag are flat: a two-dimensional graphic image. The flag on this 19th century fabric was fluttering in the wind. I started looking for pictures of old flags with a similar elegance and movement. At the same time, Candace sent me a postcard from a museum in New England of an American flag, very much in the folk-art tradition, and suggested it as an idea for a needle-point kit. We were clearly heading in the same direction, and working on a variety of source material, Candace soon produced this lovely version. It reminds me of the American flag you see in movies when the U.S. cavalry rides to the rescue.

The Stars and Stripes dates back to the Continental Congress of June 14, 1777, which "Resolved, that the Flag of the United States be thirteen stripes alternate red and white, that the Union be thirteen stars white on a blue field, representing a constellation." The red, white, and blue colors were adopted from the old colonial East India Company ensign and were the same colors found in the British flag. The 13 states of the original Union stretched up the Eastern seaboard from South Carolina to New Hampshire, and as new states joined, a new star was added to the flag. The original idea was to increase the stripes too, but when the total reached 18, it was clear that the flag would become alarmingly long. So Congress enacted a law on April 4, 1818, reducing the stripes permanently to the original 13, with stars alone to be added as new states joined the Union. The last star to be added was Hawaii's in July 1960.

O say, can you see, by the dawn's early light,
What so proudly we hail'd at the twilight's last gleaming?
Whose broad stripes and bright stars, thro' the perilous fight,
O'er the ramparts we watch'd, were so gallantly streaming?
And the rockets' red glare, the bombs bursting in air,
Gave proof thro' the night that our flag was still there.
O say, does that star-spangled banner yet wave
O'er the land of the free and the home of the brave?

This is the stirring first verse of "The Star-Spangled Banner," written by Francis Scott Key in 1814 during the War of 1812 while he was captured aboard a British ship. It marks the real beginning of national devotion to the flag, and the patriotic song was officially adopted as the national anthem of the United States in March 1931.

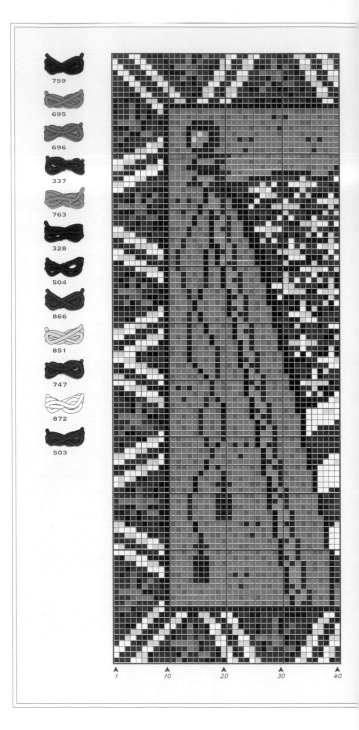

759
695
696
337
763
328
504
866
851
747
872
503

1   10   20   30   40

PREVIOUS PAGES: CANDACE STITCHES HER OWN NATION'S FLAG WITH LOVE, AFFECTION, AND A PAINSTAKING ATTENTION TO DETAIL. SHE HAS COPED BRILLIANTLY WITH THE STARS, AND THE BACKGROUND COLOR WAS WORKED AND REWORKED UNTIL SHE WAS HAPPY. THE ROPE AND TASSELS GIVE IT ITS PEDIGREE.

CANVAS: 10-gauge

STITCH: Half-cross or continental

DESIGN AREA: 15½ × 11 inches

YARN: Appleton tapestry yarn or Paternayan

Shade	Appleton	Paternayan	
Rose Pink	759	900	2 skeins
Honeysuckle Yellow	695	732	5 skeins
Honeysuckle Yellow	696	740	2 skeins
Drab Green	337	451	2 skeins
Biscuit	763	434	1 skein
Bright China Blue	747	500	3 skeins
Scarlet	504	950	2 skeins
Coral	866	850	2 skeins
Custard Yellow	851	D541	2 skeins
Dull Marine Blue	328	510	3 skeins
Pastel Yellow	872	715	4 skeins
Scarlet	503	951	2 skeins

LILY-PAD FROG

Unknown to themselves, frogs and pigs are cult creatures. Wc have learned this from experience in our business. Requests for frogs and pigs to stitch head our list. They may not be overwhelming in numbers, these piggy and froggy folk, but they are passionate in pursuit of their subject. Frog freaks collect anything with a frog on it, and a similar ardor animates the swine lover. So it was only a matter of time before Britain's leading animal stitcher would have a crack at one of them, and Kaffe Fassett went for the frog. What a dashing figure he cuts. Crouching in slippery splendor, poised to leap from his lily pad, he is a compressed coil of energy and must be one of Kaffc's most lifelike creations. The shading and use of color to evoke that lubricious sheen are a tour de force, and the strong, bold outline could only be Kaffe's. The frog is stitched with eloquent authority on 8-gauge canvas, with

WITHOUT DOUBT, A KAFFE FASSETT CLASSIC — A CONFIDENCE OF COLOR AND SCALE THAT SWEEPS ALL BEFORE IT. THIS FROG BREATHES ENERGY AND LIFE.

only 11 shades of yarn. With so few colors on such a wide-gauged canvas, this needlepoint shows, once again, that good design can be achieved with relative simplicity. It is the way you use your colors, not how many you have, that counts.

Why frogs and pigs? I don't really know. There is something appealing in their ugliness, I suppose – like the charm I find in postwar French cars. It's the right sort of ugliness, an endearing ugliness, unlike that of bats or rats (although even they have their followings). Whatever it is, frogs have risen a long way in public esteem. In religious paintings of the Middle Ages, they symbolized sin. They were given a devilish significance and often likened to heretics. After all, one of the plagues of Egypt was a rain of frogs. But now we have Mr. Jeremy Fisher, Kermit the Frog, and the Frog Prince. The toad may have retained his malevolent reputation, but the frog has become a perfectly respectable member of the animal kingdom. He certainly makes a fine subject for all sorts of artists and, with his extraordinary, expressive shape is particularly popular among jewelers and sculptors. Kaffe's frog is based on a hand-colored engraving of 1758 from Roesel Von Rosenhof's *Histoire Naturalis Ranarum*. In his book *Glorious Inspiration*, Kaffe says how instructive these hand-colored engravings can be. Their sharp, clear details are easily translated into other designs. Kaffe added his own lily pad, his own coloring, and a watery green background for those who prefer to stitch the design as a rectangular-shaped pillow. It can be stitched either way – as a modeled cutout or a pillow – and in the kit we provide the background yarn, so the choice is yours.

Cutouts are a very popular idea, so it seems natural that Kaffe has done a few. Too often they are cutesy, but Kaffe makes his stylish. He stitched a lovely pair of ducks like this, in drifts of hazy color, for his first book, *Glorious Needlepoint,* and returned to the theme recently with another pair in stronger tones. They allowed him to focus on the subtlety of shading found in ducks' feathers, since the eye is not distracted by any background patterning. Here again, the frog is a study in isolation, and I think it illustrates how good Kaffe is with animals. He somehow catches their spirit in a way that is hard to explain. These cutouts are humorous and fun, as well as being so well executed, and Kaffe even had plans at one time for stitching a life-size, cutout cow. A distinctive feature of nearly all his work is its boldness. I have used that word before, and it applies to his flowers or vegetables in the same way it applies to his animals or shells. It reflects his personality. There is no halfway with Kaffe. Whenever he stitches, he stitches with

conviction, and as the years go by, this characteristic becomes more emphatic.

When Kaffe Fassett first used an 8-gauge rug canvas to stitch pillow covers (for his fruits in *Glorious Needlepoint*), there was a chorus of disapproval from "professional" needleworkers. The more experienced a needlework designer, the finer the canvas. That had always been the accepted progression, based on the belief that needlework design was as much about technical expertise as artistic flair. For Kaffe to suddenly stride in the opposite direction was a startling move. He did so for two reasons. First, stitching on a wider gauge of canvas is quicker and more immediate. The pattern developed visually before your very eyes, making it more exciting. The second reason concerned his technical, artistic skill. Kaffe was able, at this stage, to convey the subtleties of movement and tone on this wider gauge of canvas. There are very few designers who can. Worked in these bold stitches, the design has the balance and delicacy of petitpoint.

CANVAS: 8-gauge

STITCH: Half-cross or continental

DESIGN AREA: 20 × 15 inches

YARN: Paternayan

Shade	Paternayan	
Black	221	3 skeins
Forest Green	601	4 skeins
Leaf Green	692	4 skeins
Leaf Green	693	4 skeins
Pale Spring Green	635	7 skeins
Pale Yellow	726	2 skeins
Pale Pink	935	2 skeins
Dark Brown	410	1 skein
Medium Brown	433	2 skeins
Lime Yellow	762	2 skeins
Peacock Blue	521	11 skeins

Chart overleaf.

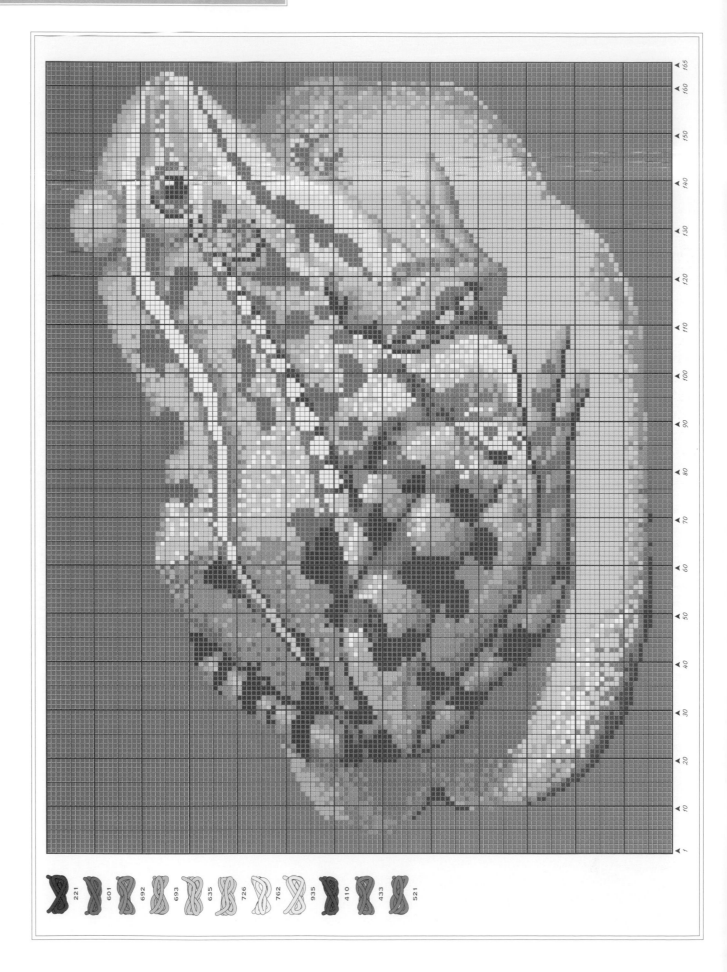

221 601 692 693 635 726 762 935 410 433 521

NOTES

Alison McDonnell's "Notes" tied for first prize in a competition we ran at the Glasgow School of Art in Scotland. Like many of the best things in life, this event came about by accident. I was having lunch with Patrick Gottelier, who runs Artwork, the knitwear company. Barbara Santos-Shaw, the head of printed textiles at Glasgow, was visiting his studio that day with a group of her students. She suggested that we put up a prize and run some sort of competition for her students to design a needlepoint kit. The idea, admittedly, had her backing, but I was amazed how enthusiastically it was received by the students. The competition was open to any second-year student, and nearly all took part. There were also requests from final-year students to participate, and a number of them did.

Ten years ago, if I had offered a prize to textile students at any art college to design a needlepoint kit, I would have been lucky to get one interested party. Such an undertaking would have been way beneath their dignity – too commercial and, in their eyes, too pedestrian. The Glasgow competition illustrates the change in profile needlework has undergone. It also illustrates a changed attitude in artistic circles to the crafts generally. Since the "designer" 1980's, when everything down to a cigarette lighter was "designed," the mood has changed. Students are now less interested in designing for mass production, and the unique object is once again

chic. The Conran Shop in London – always a good barometer in such matters – is currently full of mass-produced furniture designed to give the impression that each piece is different: a series of craftsman-made originals. The era of matte black, chrome, and stainless steel is now over, and with its passing, the crafts have gained a new respectability.

I was impressed by the way Alison approached her task. She, like nearly all the other students, had never stitched or designed a needlepoint before. The brief allowed for artwork to be presented in whatever form the competitor felt most comfortable with. Alison decided that she needed to learn how to stitch to really understand the possibilities of this new medium, and she did just that. She then proceeded to stitch this design, laboriously unpicking and reworking sections over and over again. Her painstaking attention to detail paid off. The loose style of the pillow, with its collaged composition, is counterbalanced by the fine detail of the stitching (look at the notes in the border) and the subtle, sophisticated use of color. Alison quickly realized that in almost any type of needlework, design yarns work up best when shaded softly, and the differing shades of brown stripes, blend beautifully with the 1950's mustards, oranges, and blues. Here is an excellent example of why it is always worth trying something new, and I hope we can organize similar competitions in the future.

OVERLEAF: A PRIZE-WINNING DESIGN FROM THE
GLASGOW SCHOOL OF ART, WHERE WE RAN A COMPETITION TO
ENCOURAGE YOUNG DESIGNERS TO TRY OUT NEEDLEPOINT.
MANY OF THE OTHER SUBMISSIONS WERE EQUALLY EXCITING.

The idea of employing notes and sheet music in needlework has more mileage to it. I like the way Alison McDonnell incorporates it into her overall collage, but there are many other possibilities. A simple and effective one is to stitch musical symbols straight. A piano stool of sheet music in charcoal gray and white was suggested by Jacqueline Coleman, who runs our shop, and you could stitch a highly original pillow in the same way. Sheet music creates the most fascinating patterns. It is one of the few ways to stitch in only two colors without getting bored. A theme to explore, perhaps?

CANVAS: 12-gauge

STITCH: Half-cross or continental

DESIGN AREA: 20 × 20 inches

YARN: Anchor tapisserie or Paternayan

Shade	Anchor	Paternayan	
Priest Gray	9768	221	7 skeins
Dusty Pink	8368	923	1 skein
Salmon Pink	8306	864	2 skeins
Rust Orange	8162	851	4 skeins
Flame Red	8196	821	1 skein
Dusty Pink	8366	923	1 skein
Sky Blue	8824	502	2 skeins
Sky Blue	8820	503	3 skeins
Cornflower Blue	8686	545	1 skein
Lime	9274	671	4 skeins
Heraldic Gold	9282	760	2 skeins
Old Gold	8012	263	1 skein
Cinnamon	9388	442	3 skeins
Cinnamon	9386	443	3 skeins
Khaki	9324	444	2 skeins
Rust Orange	8168	810	3 skeins
Cathedral Blue	8792	511	1 skein
Cream	8004	262	16 skeins

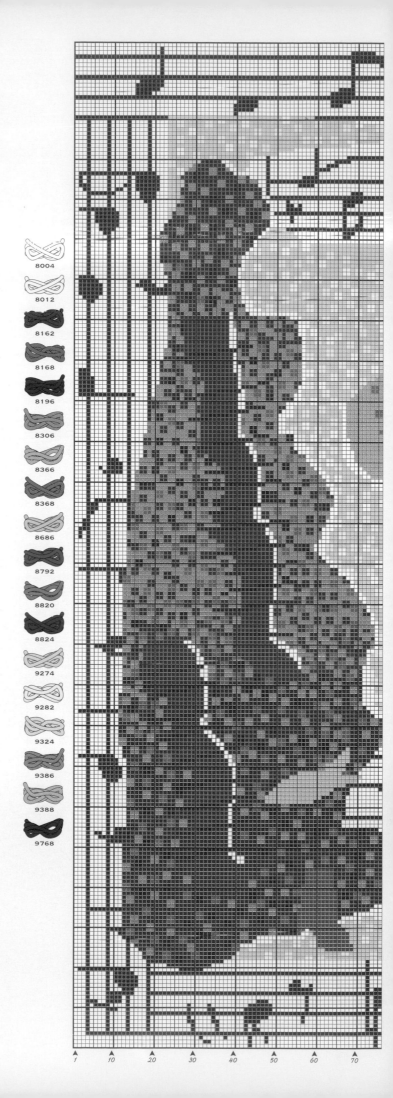

80 90 100 110 120 130 140 150 160 170 180 190 200 210 220 230 240

Chapter Five

OLD FLORALS

"Art weary? here's the place

For weariness to rest,

These flowers are herbs of grace

To cure the aching breast;

Soft beds these mossy banks

Where dewdrops only weep,

Where nature 'turns God thanks

And sings herself to sleep.

Art troubled with strife? Come hither

Here's peace and summer weather."

JOHN CLARE, "COME HITHER", 1828

ALPHABET PILLOW

Both of the last two chapters focused on the new. For this final chapter we have a group of designs that draw their inspiration from the past. Most of the designers we work with have a knowledge and appreciation of older textiles. Candace Bahouth, for example, is immersed in the medieval period, while Jill Gordon and Margaret Murton are more interested in the 17th and 18th centuries. All the designs we will see in this chapter are based on textile patterns from the past, but they are not "repro" – copies of old patterns stitched verbatim. When a contemporary designer travels back in time, it is to reexamine the achievements of previous generations in order to create something new. All of these floral designs openly profess their origins, but each is the personal work of an individual designer. The past is not copied with awed servility; it is explored. The wonderful colors and inventive ideas that crowd upon you when looking at textiles in a museum should act as a springboard for the imagination. Creative designers take ideas and inspiration from different eras. So if you are interested in needlework design, where better to start than in a museum? Kaffe Fassett based a whole book on ideas that sparked his imagination while looking at objects in the Victoria and Albert Museum in London. If you are serious about needlework design, you need to be acquainted with what has gone before. A sense of history provides an understanding of the present. Museums are not dusty, dull cathedrals of academe fit only for school field trips. They are intoxicating visual libraries assembled over many, many years. Let's use them!

We start the chapter with a design that has perhaps the faintest historical link of any. Anita Gunnett's "Alphabet Pillow" has a latticework pattern interspersed with spring flowers in pale contemporary colors. There is nothing remotely historical about that. But the use of a single central letter, transcribed from an alphabetical chart, does give this pattern a link with the past. It is reminiscent of samplers and the long needlework tradition of working individual letters and motifs for technical practice as much as for decorative effect. It is generally acknowledged that the original function of an embroidered sampler was educational. It had a twofold purpose: as an experimental exercise in learning and practice and as a record of stitch and pattern for the future.

The Elizabethan period was the second great era of English needlework, and it coincided with an addiction for all things embroidered: bags, purses, collars, gloves, handkerchiefs, jackets, bodices, smocks, vests, shirts, book bindings, carpets for tables, bedspreads, pillows, hangings, shoes – you name it, it was embroidered. A wealth of sumptuous materials drenched in a plethora of stitches trumpeted rank and status. Stitching was required at all levels of society and at all levels of technical ability. The alphabet appeared regularly in samplers because it provided practice for monogramming linen. Throughout the 17th and 18th centuries, most girls between the ages of 5 and 15 completed at least one sampler during their school years. The samplers were sometimes worked in silk and silver gilt threads, and many new stitches were used. The late 16th and early 17th centuries saw the introduction of Algerian eye or star stitch and the Hungarian, Gobelin, Florentine, rococo, long-armed cross, and eyelet stitches.

Right up until the mid-19th century, the majority of working women were still employed in three distinct occupations: agriculture, domestic service, and needleworking. During the 18th century, samplers became more pictorial, depicting biblical scenes and landscapes. They also illustrated changed attitudes in society. With the rise of Methodism and the influence of Wesley, samplers were worked expressing pious thoughts, with stitched selections from the Scriptures, devoid of decoration or embellishment. With the mechanization of textile production in the 19th century, society's requirements for embroidery and skilled embroiderers diminished. This was reflected in the declining standard of samplers. Embroidery became, at its higher end, a social grace, an exercise in concentration and dexterity, but it lost the progressive vitality of earlier times. Now we stitch reproductions of historical samplers for no better reason than we like the look of them.

A SIMPLE PATTERN WITH THE FEEL OF A SAMPLER.

WE THOUGHT IT WOULD BE A NICE CHANGE TO PRODUCE

A KIT THAT COULD BE PERSONALIZED.

| 101 | 124 | 254 | 354 | 551 | 554 | 881 | 895 |

| 104 | 253 | 352 | 471 | 552 | 843 | 892 |

The idea of this pattern is to personalize it with an initial of your choice. The central panel is left empty for this purpose. The geometric structure of the design, however, allows you to replace the individual spring flowers with other motifs if you wish. In this way the samplers can become – like so many samplers in the past – a personal scrapbook of familiar and favorite images. Many samplers from the 17th and 18th centuries, usually stitched by children, were a charming amalgam of animals, houses, trees, birds, and insects mixed in with lettering.

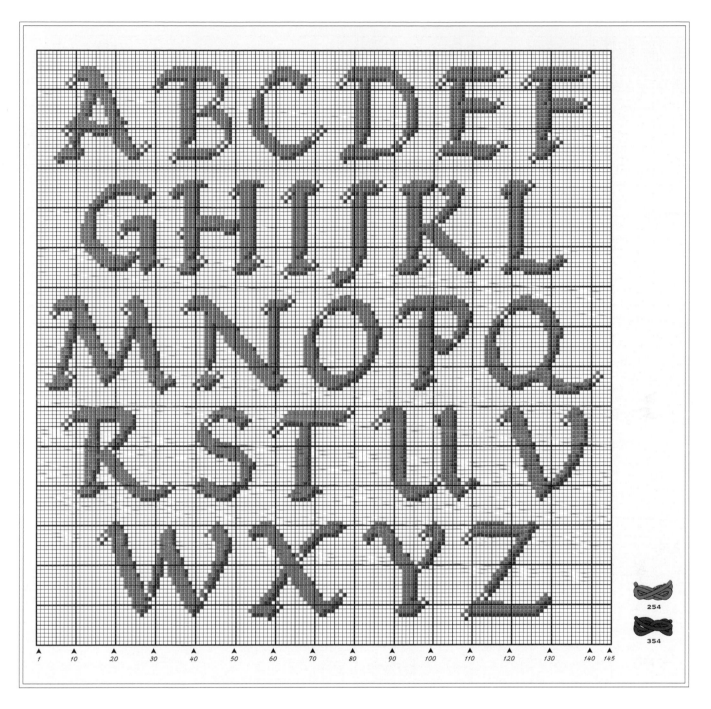

CANVAS: 12-gauge

STITCH: Half-cross or continental

DESIGN AREA: 14 × 14 inches

YARN: Appleton tapestry yarn or Paternayan

Shade	Appleton	Paternayan	
Purple	101	313	1 skein
Purple	104	312	1 skein
Terracotta	124	484	2 skeins
Grass Green	253	693	3 skeins
Grass Green	254	692	2 skeins

Shade	Appleton	Paternayan	
Gray Green	352	605	4 skeins
Gray Green	354	603	4 skeins
Autumn Yellow	471	727	3 skeins
Bright Yellow	551	773	1 skein
Bright Yellow	552	713	1 skein
Bright Yellow	554	771	1 skein
Heraldic Gold	843	733	1 skein
Pastel White	881	262	18 skeins
Hyacinth	892	313	1 skein
Hyacinth	895	310	1 skein

CHALICE OF FRUITS

This design from Neil McCallum has a "country manor" flavor. What does this term conjure up? As with so many useful, generalized, and inclusive classifications, it is difficult to be precise. In England we would probably think of Colefax and Fowler interiors, the National Trust, Wellington boots, and Labradors. "Country manor" has as much to do with a way of life as with a particular style. But in terms of architecture and furnishings, it has a wider European dimension. In the 17th and 18th centuries, buildings and their interiors across Europe developed along broadly similar lines, with many features in common. It was a look that subsequently crossed the Atlantic. The Palladian proportions of James Hoban's White House, the pillared facades of plantation houses in the South, or the Georgian town architecture of Boston and New York look as familiar to a European as they do to an American.

The 17th and 18th centuries were the centuries, above all others, that saw the commercial expansion of Europe. Huge wealth was accumulated by energetic, enterprising, and determined men, and this new merchant prosperity spread itself widely. The last vestiges of the medieval world, with its narrowly prescribed structures of power and patronage, were transformed into a broader economic pluralism. The foundations of the Western world were laid: the creation of a European bourgeoisie, the emergence of the professions, and the growing importance of money within the social hierarchy. In varying degrees this process happened across Europe, and much of the new wealth found its way into country estates. Owning land became an important avenue to a rise in social rank, and once you had some land, you needed a fine house built on it, which itself needed to be lavishly furnished.

The medieval lord had ruled by personal contact with his supporters. This meant traveling with his retinue from one great house to the next. Tapestries, folding beds and chairs, chests, embroidered cushions and hangings came along too. With the passing of this way of life, a house became a more settled affair – a home. The interior furnishings were conceived along with the architecture of the building. Interiors were planned as static set pieces. This gave scope for finer detail and the greater elaboration of furniture and furnishings in general. Architects and pattern books traveled extensively across Europe, and a new classical style emerged that affected all aspects of a building. It was common for a French architect in the 17th century to insist on controlling every aspect of the interior – the application of the Renaissance ideals of unity.

With this greater emphasis on visual coordination, recurrent motifs and decorative devices popped up in an almost interchangeable manner. From what source might Neil McCallum have taken his stylized vase and fruits? It could have been a plaster frieze, a fabric pattern, a piece of furniture. It is impossible to say. Floral sprays, garlanded repeats, classical urns, cartouches, or armorial compositions are not associated with a particular product. They are associated

with a period, and Neil's pillow is at home there. Being such a universal style for so long, enduring designs like these blend in happily today. From the mid-17th century, less time was spent in embroidering pillows and cushions. More attention was paid to their presentation, with trimmings and fringes in prominence. From about 1630, it was common for many fine cushions to be finished off with four large tassels, one at each corner, and we decided to do the same with "Chalice of Fruits."

NEIL MCCALLUM (PICTURED OPPOSITE) OPTS FOR RICH COLORS WITH THIS TRADITIONAL PATTERN. IT WORKS IN A GRAND SETTING OR IN THE RELATIVE SIMPLICITY CHOSEN HERE BY ZÖE AND TIM HILL.

This is a pattern to try with different colored backgrounds. Darker ones would look good: navy blue, a deep red, or chocolate brown. As you can see from the list of shade numbers below, Neil has gone to town on the detail. You could simplify a little if you wished, but that would be a shame. This design comes as close to the feel of a hand-painted canvas as a printed kit ever will. That is partly because of McCallum's choice of a 12-gauge canvas for what is quite a large pillow cover, but it is mainly because of the number of colors. So many colors enable a wealth of subtle shade changes, which are normally associated with hand-painted canvases.

CANVAS: 12-gauge

STITCH: Half-cross or continental

DESIGN AREA: 20 × 14 inches

YARN: Appleton tapestry yarn or Paternayan

Shade	Appleton	Paternayan	
Purple	103	312	1 skein
Terracotta	128	920	1 skein
Dull Rose Pink	144	912	2 skeins
Dull Rose Pink	145	911	2 skeins
Olive Green	243	642	3 skeins
Grass Green	253	693	2 skeins
Jacobean Green	295	601	2 skeins
Red Fawn	301	435	2 skeins
Brown Olive	315	D511	2 skeins
Cornflower	465	540	2 skeins
Autumn Yellow	471	727	2 skeins
Autumn Yellow	474	725	2 skeins
Autumn Yellow	475	723	1 skein
Autumn Yellow	476	722	1 skein
Early English Green	548	600	2 skeins
Paprika	721	872	1 skein
Rose Pink	757	902	2 skeins
Rose Pink	759	900	2 skeins
Biscuit Brown	765	412	2 skeins
Coral	863	862	1 skein
Pastel White	882	263	18 skeins
Pastel Lavender	883	D147	1 skein
Hyacinth	894	312	2 skeins
Golden Brown	903	442	1 skein
Fawn	916	450	2 skeins
Putty Grounding	985	463	2 skeins
Charcoal	998	221	1 skein

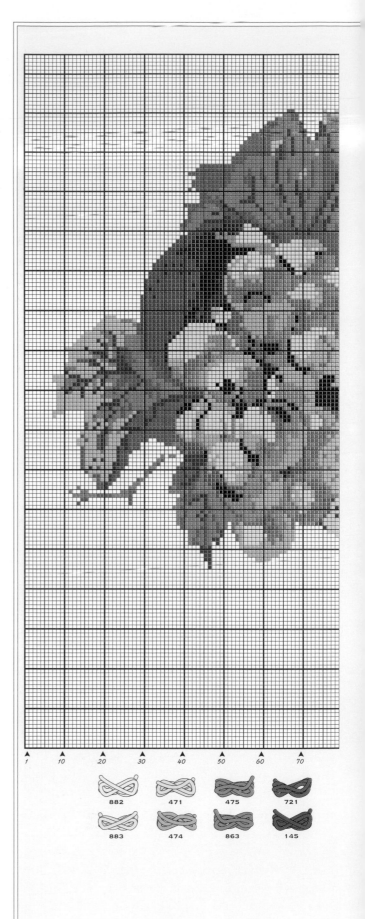

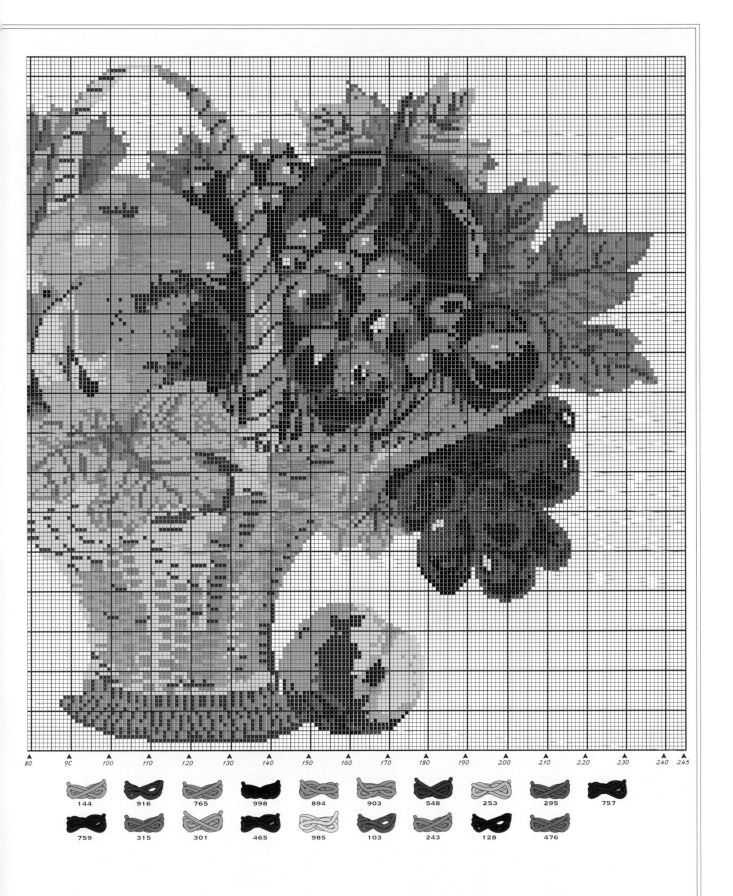

A MINI TRIO

There has been great demand recently for smaller kits to stitch. In general, needlepoint kits have been getting larger, and not only ours. Designers usually like to work on a larger scale. It gives much greater scope for real design, and as a result, Ehrman has been producing more hangings and rugs than usual. But larger kits do take a long time to stitch, and they are expensive. They are also rather cumbersome, and it was inevitable that there should, at some stage, be a counterreaction, with people looking for simpler, quicker, cheaper projects that could fit easily into a bag for taking along to work or when traveling. Two years ago Glorafilia produced a series of four blue-and-white mini designs based on china patterns. They were different, fresh, and appealing, and I wasn't a bit surprised to hear how well they sold. Word travels fast in the small world of the needlework trade and, always ready to cash in on a trend, here we are, a little later, with our own offering! I think Anita Gunnett has been wise to choose a 14-gauge canvas for her designs. It allows for some detail. The charm of embroidery on a small scale lies in its detail. When you think of embroidered handkerchiefs, gloves, or purses, you think of the jewel-like quality of petit point. Kaffe Fassett has some beautiful slippers in his new book, also worked on 14-gauge canvas. I think there is no escaping fine canvas for designs of this size, and anyway, it makes a pleasant change from the long stitch or 7-gauge rug canvas of our larger kits.

We first met Anita at the Royal School of Needlework. When we started our business, our two principal designers were Kaffe Fassett and the Royal School of Needlework. It is hard to think of two more contrasting styles, but that was partly the idea. We felt that we needed to balance Kaffe's innovative, modern designs with a more traditional look if we were to appeal to a wide audience. We have always looked for good design wherever we can find it. The style is immaterial; what matters is the intrinsic quality of the work. The Royal School was sitting on a wealth of archive material, including original designs for canvas work by Walter Crane and Burne-Jones. It was criminally under-utilized, and we commissioned the school's design department to produce a series of kits for us, many of which drew on this rich body of archive material. The Royal School has always been a curious hybrid of an institution. Its primary function has traditionally been textile conservation and restoration, along with commissioned work, much of it ceremonial. At the same time, it has sporadically produced its own commercial designs, either as painted canvases or as kits, but in a rather haphazard, unplanned fashion. This is a shame because the school has an interesting store of patterns. This year it has started to market a range of kits in a serious attempt to do something about this. This may mean competition for the rest of us, but it should be welcomed by needleworkers generally. If handled properly this time, it will resurrect a fine collection of design that has been lying dormant for much too long. It should enhance the choice of kits available.

Anita was working in the Royal School's design department in the early 1980's and was responsible for a number of our kits. Another designer working there at the time was Susan Skeen. They both went freelance, and we have continued to work with them, on and off, ever since. It is very nice to have some new patterns from Anita, and these small canvases can be used in a number of ways. They make attractive little pictures in their own right, almost like textile fragments, or they can be bordered to make small pillows. A group of them could be combined to make a larger patchwork, or they could even be used as appliqués on clothes. A German magazine ran a reader offer last year of Candace Bahouth's "Cherubs." I was astonished to see how they had used it. They had cut it into sections and patched a jean jacket with it. With a little imagination, it is remarkable what you can do with a piece of needlepoint.

THREE SMALLER CANVASES FROM ANITA GUNNETT:
CHEAPER, QUICKER, AND LESS BULKY. WE HAVE
HAD AN INCREASING NUMBER OF REQUESTS
FOR KITS OF THIS SIZE.

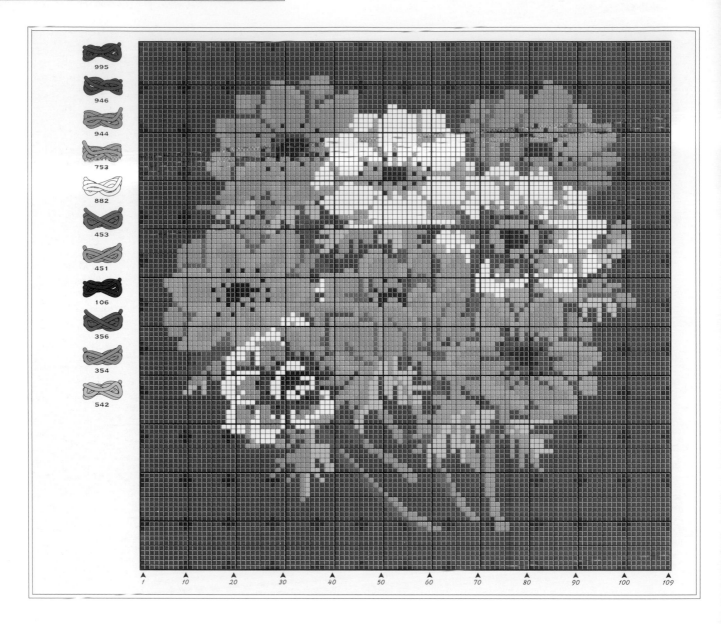

These three small designs could be worked up as bags. In her book, *Medieval Needlepoint*, Candace Bahouth produced a range of smaller designs, on finer canvas, for evening bags with metallic thread and beads. This added sparkle. There are catalogs of beads available that offer a huge selection of colors and materials, and these beads can be easily overstitched.

ANEMONES SQUARE

CANVAS: 14-gauge

STITCH: Half-cross or continental

DESIGN AREA: 8 × 8 inches

YARN: Appleton tapestry yarn or Paternayan

Shade	Appleton	Paternayan	
Cherry Red	995	940	6 skeins
Bright Rose Pink	946	903	1 skein
Bright Rose Pink	944	904	2 skeins
Rose Pink	753	D281	2 skeins
Pastel White	882	263	2 skeins
Mauve	453	302	1 skein
Mauve	451	323	1 skein
Purple	106	320	2 skeins
Gray Green	356	601	1 skein
Gray Green	354	603	3 skeins
Early English Green	542	653	1 skein

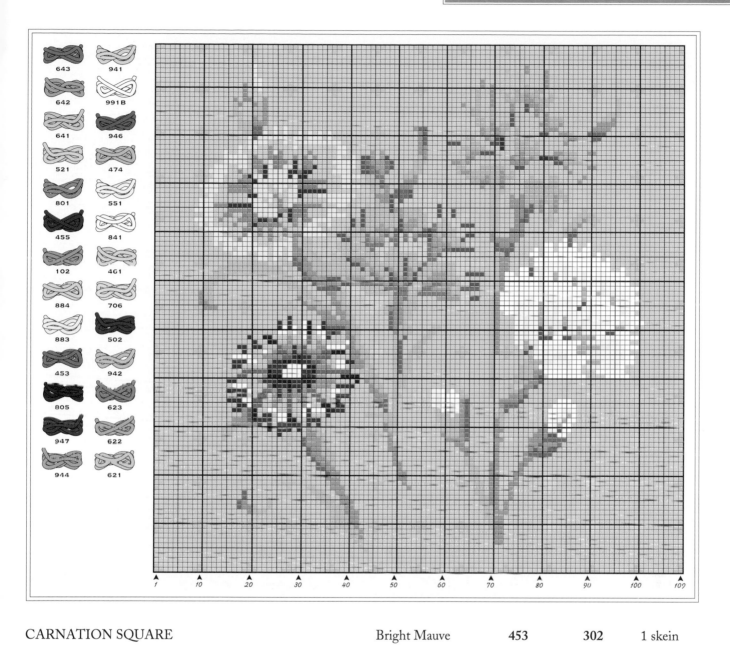

CARNATION SQUARE

CANVAS: 14-gauge

STITCH: Half-cross or continental

DESIGN AREA: 8 × 8 inches

YARN: Appleton tapestry yarn or Paternayan

Shade	Appleton	Paternayan	
Peacock Blue	643	602	1 skein
Peacock Blue	642	D546	1 skein
Peacock Blue	641	523	1 skein
Turquoise	521	525	1 skein
Fuchsia	801	353	1 skein
Bright Mauve	455	301	1 skein
Purple	102	312	1 skein
Pastel Lilac	884	314	1 skein
Pastel Heather	883	D147	1 skein
Bright Mauve	453	302	1 skein
Fuchsia	805	350	1 skein
Bright Rose Pink	947	902	1 skein
Bright Rose Pink	944	904	1 skein
Bright Rose Pink	941	934	1 skein
Bright White	991B	260	1 skein
Bright Rose Pink	946	903	1 skein
Autumn Yellow	474	725	1 skein
Bright Yellow	551	773	1 skein
Heraldic Gold	841	704	1 skein
Cornflower	461	564	8 skeins
Flesh Tint	706	492	2 skeins
Scarlet	502	841	1 skein
Bright Rose Pink	942	933	1 skein
Flamingo	623	833	1 skein
Flamingo	622	834	1 skein
Flamingo	621	835	1 skein

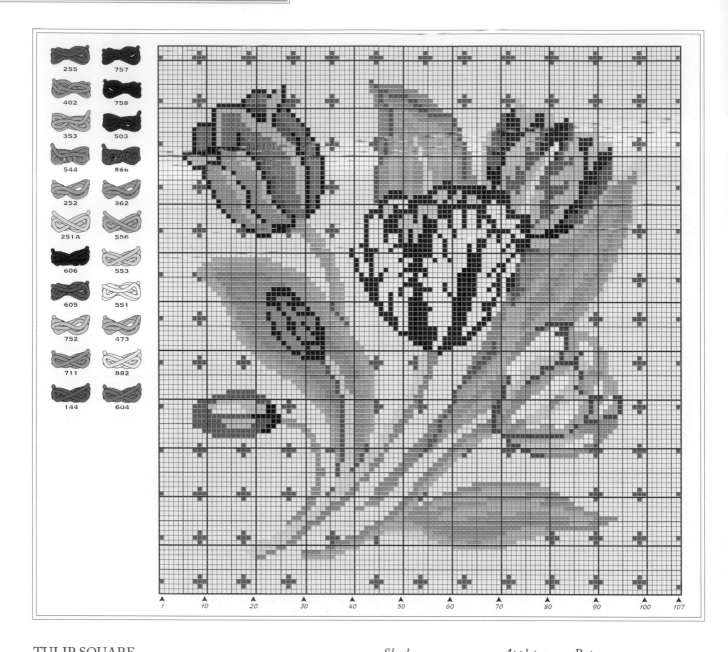

TULIP SQUARE

CANVAS: 14-gauge

STITCH: Half-cross or continental

DESIGN AREA: 8 × 8 inches

YARN: Appleton tapestry yarn or Paternayan

Shade	Appleton	Paternayan	
Grass Green	255	651	1 skein
Sea Green	402	612	1 skein
Gray Green	353	604	1 skein
Early English Green	544	692	1 skein
Grass Green	252	694	1 skein
Grass Green	251A	653	1 skein
Mauve	606	310	1 skein

Shade	Appleton	Paternayan	
Mauve	605	311	1 skein
Rose Pink	752	945	1 skein
Wine Red	711	914	1 skein
Dull Rose Pink	144	912	1 skein
Rose Pink	757	902	1 skein
Rose Pink	758	901	1 skein
Scarlet	503	951	1 skein
Coral	866	850	1 skein
Coral	862	854	1 skein
Bright Yellow	556	813	1 skein
Bright Yellow	553	772	1 skein
Bright Yellow	551	773	1 skein
Autumn Yellow	473	732	1 skein
Pastel White	882	263	7 skeins
Mauve	604	312	1 skein

SAVONNERIE

Jill Gordon called this design "Savonnerie" for its color rather than its composition. The designs of the Savonnerie carpets tended to be grand and formal in contrast to the more domestic patterns of Aubusson carpets. The name Savonnerie came from the original building that housed carpet production in Chaillot, France, which was a former soap factory. Every month a painter from the Royal Academy inspected designs and gave drawing lessons for the design staff. With the explosion of royal building taking place, the Savonnerie's production was reserved for the crown. In addition to all the work undertaken for the Louvre, furnishing was also required for Versailles, where the court was installed in 1682. During this period all design was supervised by Charles Lebrun, and it was intended to reflect the glories of the age. A uniform style had emerged, with garlands of flowers and bold leaf scrolls set against black or brown backgrounds. The practice of having an artist in charge of design continued throughout the 18th century, with Lebrun being succeeded by Belin de Fontenay in 1667. He had been a flower painter at the Gobelins and brought with him a lighter touch. By the mid-18th century, rococo devices were appearing – palm trees, shells, bat wings, and fleur-de-lis – and also lighter colors. Pink, yellow, pale blue, and white replaced the earlier black and deep brown backgrounds. Jill's colors are nearer to this period of the Savonnerie's production.

Jill's colors are beautifully soft. They succeed in looking like the bleached colors of old textiles, where the passage of time and the effects of the sun have taken their toll. They are brought into relief, just where they might have merged themselves away into a vapor, with the crisp blue of a summer sky. Much too often, backgrounds are a single matte color. Just look what the patterned background adds to this design. It puts it in a different league, adding depth and perspective. Jill Gordon, like so many of our designers, started life as a painter. The slightly off-centered combination of fruits and flowers, the muted drifts of attenuated color, and the mottled blues of the sky, all remind me of her watercolors and give this pattern its relaxed, easy air.

CANVAS: 10-gauge

STITCH: Half-cross or continental

DESIGN AREA: 16 × 16 inches

YARN: Appleton tapestry yarn or Paternayan

Shade	Appleton	Paternayan	
Dull Rose Pink	141	924	3 skeins
Flame Red	205	872	3 skeins
Drab Green	332	643	6 skeins
Drab Green	334	642	4 skeins
Drab Green	341	644	2 skeins
Honeysuckle Yellow	692	754	6 skeins
Honeysuckle Yellow	693	734	5 skeins
Bright China Blue	743	561	3 skeins
Bright China Blue	746	560	3 skeins
Rose Pink	754	913	3 skeins
Rose Pink	757	902	2 skeins
Biscuit Brown	766	D419	3 skeins
Pastel White	882	263	4 skeins
Pastel Blue	886	564	2 skeins
Golden Brown	902	442	6 skeins

This design really does manage to capture the faded feel of an older fabric. As a result, it could be used in a number of ways. Sections of woven tapestries are sometimes used to cover folders or binders, and "Savonnerie" would be a good design for that. It would make a lovely needlepoint bag or stool seat and would go well on a round footstool. Starting at the center of the chart, simply mark the area you need to stitch, depending on the measurements of your footstool. Although you will cut into the design, it doesn't matter. Because the design is based on fabric patterns, it can be used, like fabric, for all kinds of upholstery.

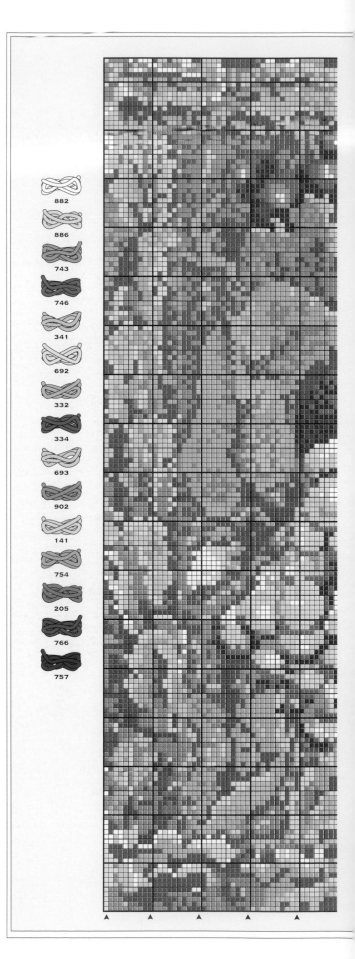

SUMMER

argaret Murton's time machine has taken her back to the late 16th century. In the tapestries of Brussels and Mortlake, a notable feature of these hangings was the borders. Garlanded festoons of flowers and vegetables struggle for space with tumbling cascades of fruit. Wheat sheaves and the gifts of Mother Nature compete with swagged cornucopias for any available toehold. These borders are literally overflowing with natural produce, and initially the eye is submerged under a tidal wave of detail. But then, they are only borders and were never intended to be viewed as independent designs. They are sumptuous sources of inspiration, and when people talk of the "richness of tapestry," I often think of these fecund riots.

The way Margaret Murton works illustrates how a contemporary designer uses the past. As a watercolorist, she began painting decorative florals and fruits on old wooden panels for houses in France and England. They are lovely, the wood enhancing her faded, washed use of paint. It is always a joy to receive her artwork, which normally comes as a watercolor painting. Margaret lives in Leicestershire, England, in a very attractive and still relatively unspoiled part of the country. She works from the nature that surrounds her. Her sketchbook brims with fields of daisies, honeysuckle tendrils twining through brier roses, studies of leaves and fruits, berries, and plants. These are the elements that are arranged and rearranged into her designs. As she says, her floral and fruit motifs are "found in almost all Flemish and French tapestries of the 16th and 17th centuries," but hers are her own. It is what I meant at the beginning of the chapter when I said that a contemporary designer travels back in time to reexamine the achievements of previous generations in order to create something new. The context is there, the colors are there – subdued creams, dusty golds, and pinks, Prussian and indigo blues, but the design, the actual composition, is quite new. These designs are not copies of old borders. Old borders act as the springboard for Margaret's imagination. And the same goes for all the designs in this chapter. Not one of them is a copy of an existing historical piece. They are all the original works of living artists.

Margaret would be the first to admit how difficult it is to reduce the infinite variations of paint into a selected band of roughly 20 colors. If you start from a watercolor painting, choosing your yarn colors is the next process, and it is an art in itself. Whereas Kaffe Fassett and Elian McCready stitch their color compositions as they go, Margaret works the other way around. Her challenge is to capture the color essence of her original in yarn. First of all, the design has to

be graphed into the small squares that will correspond with the reticulated nature of the canvas (I always liked the couture designer Hardy Amies's description of canvas embroidery as "filling holes with wool"). This is like trying to splinter a raindrop. The only way to start is to place a sheet of graph paper over the painting and decide what are the predominant shades in each square. We allow our designers a maximum of only 25 colors, and we get upset if they use that many! The preferred amount is anywhere between 10 and 20. The reason is purely economic. The cost of produc-

DESIGNED TO LOOK LIKE A SECTION TAKEN FROM THE BORDER OF A 17TH-CENTURY EUROPEAN WOVEN HANGING, "SUMMER" HAS AN ADDED TOUCH OF LIGHTER COLOR TO SOFTEN THINGS A LITTLE.

tion rises disproportionately when you go beyond that level. So the color in each square has to be chosen from a very restricted menu. This process then goes back and forth.

| 1 | 10 | 20 | 30 | 40 | 50 | 60 | 70 | 80 | 90 | 100 | 110 | 120 | 130 | 140 |

| 157 | 642 | 521 | 923 | 886 | 203 | 621 | 222 | 205 | 125 |

Working within the maximum prescribed total, the designer may find halfway through, for example, that two or three more greens are needed. This may mean sacrificing a couple of blues and one of those pinks, which, in a pinch, one can live without. But now the section just completed must be redesigned to accord with the new palette. It is a skill, and it is all a matter of balance, judgment, and compromise.

Finally, the actual selection of the yarns takes place. Here the designer chooses 10 or 20 shades from a range of more than 300. These need to recapture the original feel of the watercolor as closely as possible, but they also need to work comfortably together when stitched. At this point some experimental stitching of different sections takes place until the final formula is decided. There is a lot more to choosing

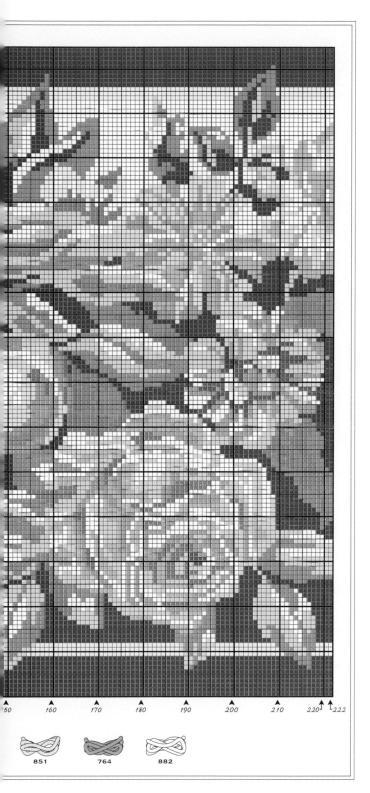

color restrictions. The subtlety and beauty that can be achieved with 50 colors, as opposed to 20, is immeasurably greater. This is one of the frustrations of producing printed canvases. I am always delighted when I hear that one of our designers has won a private commission. I know that, with no restriction on color, he or she will, in all probability, produce something really interesting. If you are planning to stitch your own design, and particularly if you start with a watercolor, I would advise you to let it rip on color. Each hole has to be "filled with yarn," so why not make as many of them as different as possible? I am sure you will find the shading of flowers or fruits a lot easier with a good range of colors, and when you get used to using a lot of color, it will seem very natural. What is unnatural is our stinginess with color. Unfortunately, to produce a needlepoint kit, it has to be so; but, therein lies the skill of our designers.

CANVAS: 12-gauge

STITCH: Half-cross or continental

DESIGN AREA: 18 × 12 inches

YARN: Appleton tapestry yarn or Paternayan

Shade	Appleton	Paternayan	
Terracotta	125	482	1 skein
Medium Blue	157	531	6 skeins
Flame Red	203	486	2 skeins
Flame Red	205	872	2 skeins
Bright Terracotta	222	933	2 skeins
Turquoise	521	525	3 skeins
Flamingo	621	835	2 skeins
Peacock Blue	642	D546	4 skeins
Biscuit Brown	764	413	2 skeins
Custard Yellow	851	D541	2 skeins
Pastel White	882	263	6 skeins
Pastel Blue	886	564	2 skeins
Dull China Blue	923	513	2 skeins

"Summer" is part of Margaret Murton's "Four Seasons" series. "Spring" was the most popular, but I have always preferred "Summer" and "Autumn." Their colors are softer, and Margaret is best when her colors merge and blend.

This pattern could almost be repeated, end to end, to produce a long runner or bell pull to hang on a wall. It would need a little creative adaptation, but it could be made to work.

colors than most people imagine: the whole design can be spoiled at the end if the yarns stitch up darker or lighter than expected. It is impossible to pick colors simply by looking at a shade card. The colors need to be worked up to test relative densities and to iron out any unexpected surprises when two colors meet side by side.

It is easy to see why designers like to work with fewer

BLOOMING ROSES

As he did for "Berlin Roses" in the first chapter, David Merry adapted this pattern from mid-19th-century charts. This design, however, has a softer feel to it, with a greater sense of motion, and we toned the colors down further to match the mood. On the original Berlin Woolwork chart, more than 50 colors were used, so the process of thinning them out was painstaking. To get the colors right, you can't cut corners, and if you are doing this for your own project, you will need to work up sections to test how your colors react together.

Many needlecraft stores sell hand-painted canvases and yarns separately. For those with a good eye and a little self-confidence, this is a chance to select and combine their own colors. But the majority of stitchers do not have such self-confidence. When picking shades of yarn for their hand-painted canvas, they rely on the advice of the store manager. It was Candace Bahouth who pointed this out to me. It seemed shocking to her how casually colors are chosen – reds, yellows, greens, or blues plucked almost at random to match the painted color squares on a canvas. None of these color combinations are tested, and the results are bound to be hit or miss affair. A store manager may or may not have a good eye for color mixing. A kit offers little flexibility, and the quality of a printed canvas is undoubtedly inferior to that of a painted canvas, but at least you know that the colors will work up as expected. When you buy a kit, you buy the hours of agonizing and experimentation that lie behind the designer's choice of yarns.

CANVAS: 12-gauge

STITCH: Half-cross or continental

DESIGN AREA: 14 × 12 inches

YARN: Appleton tapestry yarn or Paternayan

Shade	Appleton	Paternayan	
White	991	261	1 skein
Flame Red	202	406	2 skeins
Flame Red	203	486	1 skein
Terracotta	124	484	2 skeins
Rose Pink	752	945	1 skein
Rose Pink	754	913	2 skeins
Bright Terracotta	225	931	2 skeins
Scarlet	504	950	3 skeins
Terracotta	128	920	2 skeins
Golden Brown	901	443	1 skein
Chocolate	182	463	1 skein
Red Fawn	302	412	1 skein
Chocolate	185	431	1 skein

Sea Green	401	613	2 skeins	Bright Peacock Green	832	662	2 skeins
Peacock Green	642	D546	1 skein	Medium Olive Green	342	643	2 skeins
Jacobean Green	293	603	2 skeins	Drab Green	333	643	2 skeins
Peacock Green	647	660	1 skein	Drab Green	335	D511	2 skeins
Peacock Green	641	523	1 skein	*Background (choose one color)*			
Olive Green	242	652	2 skeins	Pastel White	881	262	10 skeins
Medium Olive Green	345	642	1 skein	Charcoal	998	221	10 skeins

AUBUSSON

And so we reach the final design in this book, which comes from Candace Bahouth. Her Aubusson roses pattern works as a chair cushion or pillow cover. The colors, although derived from the subdued, chalky tones of 18th-century carpets, have a distinctive sparkle of their own. The little touches of lilac and pale green, along with the powder blues, add a freshness to this traditional design.

When looking at Jill Gordon's "Savonnerie," I mentioned Aubusson carpets. The designs of the Savonnerie, destined as they were for the royal palaces of France, had a grandeur unsuited to most domestic interiors. Emblems, crests, and weapons for the nobility set the tone for many Savonnerie hangings, whereas Aubusson carpets tended to feature a central motif surrounded by garlands or scatterings of flowers. Ribbons and bunches of flowers decorated plain, simple colored backgrounds, which were usually white, pale yellow, or crimson. Most of the crimson backgrounds have now faded to crushed strawberry. If you think of Aubusson carpets, you think of light, summery colors.

Aubusson carpets differed in style from the grander Savonnerie weavings, more from necessity than choice. They were cheaper. To be cheaper, they had to use fewer colors and a bolder, less detailed configuration of pattern; a less showy style of design developed, largely as a result of cost restrictions. The painter Louis-Joseph Le Lorrain created a real innovation in design with his model *à la grande mosaique* in 1753, praised for its simplicity, which did not distract the eye from the furniture in the room. Although Louis XV ordered carpets for the château at Choisy, and Napoleon commissioned pile carpets for Versailles and the

CANDACE BAHOUTH SHOWS AN INSTINCTIVE FEEL FOR
THE POWDERY, CRUSHED COLORS OF AUBUSSON CARPETS. THIS
CHAIR CUSHION IS A ROMANTIC DESIGN OF SOFT EDGES AND
BLURRED FOCUS. "BLOOMING ROSES" BY DAVID MERRY (PAGE
130–31) WOULD FIT IN WELL ANYWHERE.

Petit Trianon, most of the factory's output supplied the needs of France's growing bourgeoisie. Aubusson carpets sometimes come up for sale at auction, and if they are in reasonable condition, will cost between $16,000 and $32,000. They have remained consistently popular because they are so easy to live with.

CANVAS: 10-gauge

STITCH: Half-cross or continental

DESIGN AREA: 20 × 20 inches

YARN: Appleton tapestry yarn or Paternayan

Shade	Appleton	Paternayan	
Terracotta	125	482	2 skeins
Medium Blue	151	203	3 skeins
Medium Blue	152	514	3 skeins
Bright Terracotta	225	931	2 skeins
Olive Green	242	652	2 skeins
Dull Maine Blue	322	513	3 skeins
Medium Olive Green	343	643	2 skeins
Autumn Yellow	471	727	2 skeins
Early English Grass Green	542	653	2 skeins
Mauve	601	325	1 skein
Mauve	603	323	1 skein
Peacock Blue	646	661	1 skein
Honeysuckle Yellow	695	732	1 skein
Flesh Tint	706	492	2 skeins
Rose Pink	753	D281	2 skeins
Rose Pink	755	D275	2 skeins
Custard Yellow	851	D541	9 skeins
Bright Peacock Blue	853	511	2 skeins
Pastel White	881	262	3 skeins

This pattern was always envisaged by Candace as a pillow as well as a cushion. We have photographed it as a chair cushion because we don't have any others in this book, but it would work just as well stitched as a pillow. Your chair will need to be the right shape for this pattern. It would spoil the design if you lost some of the ribbon border so measure carefully before you start. On a pillow, the sur-rounding ribbon border finishes the design off well. The soft colors would go with a wide variety of home furnishings, and at 20 inches square, the pillow is a comfortable but manageable size.

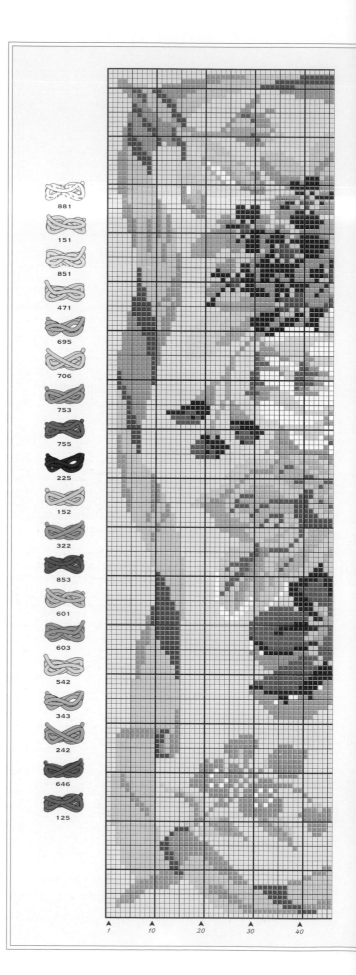

50 60 70 80 90 100 110 120 130 140 150 160 170 176

TECHNIQUES

Every design in this book can be easily stitched if you have the will and determination to do so. After you have mastered the basic stitch, it is simply a matter of repeating it and covering your canvas. The challenge with all these designs is in the shading, where a phenomenal spectrum of tone and color has been used. Using a limited palette of colors, mixing and blending – as opposed to using hard blocks of color – the designers have created glorious patterns. Designing like this can be a tedious business, but it is also true to say that many Ehrman customers welcome the opportunity to tackle something a little more challenging. Until the mid-1980's, all needlepoint kits were consciously designed for color-block printing. With the publication of Kaffe Fassett's *Glorious Needlepoint* in 1987, we embarked (rather fearfully) on more ambitious kit designs, where shading played a greater part. We were always aware of the potential problems involved, but on balance it has been worthwhile. With such complex shading, it is essential that only one stitch be used. We have always kept our kits restricted to half-cross or continental stitch for this very reason. The complexity is in the color, and adding different stitches to detailed areas of pattern is impractical. Although variation in stitches adds textural dimension to a design, in our kits it is a luxury we must forgo. If you are working one of our kits, our advice is to stick to the same stitch for anything other than a geometric border or other large area of single color.

After many hours of hard work and, we hope, enjoyment, you will have a piece of stitched fabric. When your design is completed, there is no right or wrong way to finish it. When you have put time and effort into stitching, however, it is worthwhile to finish your work in the best and most appropriate way possible. Many of the projects in this book have been made into pillows but would work equally well as hangings, chair cushions, pictures, or with the design repeated, as rugs. Remember, too, that by stitching on canvas, you are crafting a new fabric. From coarse canvas, a soft, strong, textured fabric appears, and this can be used to make practical yet decorative bags and clothing. Do not be inhibited by what you see – needlepoint has many possibilities. What you decide to do with your work can be as creative as the needlepoint itself.

EQUIPMENT

FABRICS

All of the projects in this book are worked on canvas. Originally derived from hemp or burlap, canvas is a coarse yet versatile medium, ideal for needlepoint. These days you will find linen, cotton, and some synthetic canvases. The cotton canvases are easiest to work with because they handle and wash well. Synthetic canvas tends not to be suitable for making furnishings because it is made from a lightweight plastic that retains its stiffness when stitched; it is often used for three-dimensional projects.

**MONO CANVAS
(SINGLE THREAD)**

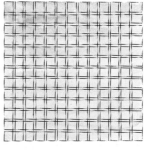

**PENELOPE CANVAS
(DOUBLE MESH)**

Canvas is available in either single or double mesh. The former, called interlock mono, is more common, but it is prone to distort when handled unless the canvas is mounted on a frame and the finished piece is blocked (see page 139). Double-mesh canvas, called Penelope, is stronger, consisting of pairs of threads woven together. This weave can be split, allowing you to work half stitches and create fine detail.

The difference between canvases is determined by the number of meshes per inch. The greater the number of meshes per inch, the finer the design. The size is referred to as the gauge. A large count can be tricky to work, and the design may take longer to grow than it would if you were working on a smaller gauge. The most frequently used canvases for working with tapestry yarn are between 10 and 16 gauge. When working with rug yarn or a thicker, coarser yarn, a smaller gauge of canvas, 7 or even 5 gauge, is used. In such a case it is advisable to use a thicker yarn because a normal four-ply tapestry yarn may not cover the canvas.

You can work the same design on all gauges, and you will find the size of your finished project will differ depending on which gauge of canvas you use.

YARNS

The projects in this book have been worked in tapestry yarns. A tapestry yarn is generally 100 percent wool. It does not stretch like a knitting yarn and is eminently stronger and more hard-wearing. The main brands used are Paternayan and Appleton, and a DMC yarn conversion chart is provided on page 142. Paternayan tapestry yarn is four-ply. You can split the strands to work in one, two, three, or four strands, as the pattern suggests. On a 14-gauge canvas, you would expect to work with a single strand.

Some of the designs use blended yarns. To blend yarn, take one strand of each color, thread them together through your needle, and work with both strands. The effect is textured and very subtle.

You can work out the amount of yarn you will need by measuring off a length of tapestry yarn and working a test section of your canvas until you run out of yarn. Count the number of stitches and subtract 20 percent. For example, if you work 40 stitches with a 15-inch single strand, then subtract 20 percent of 40 stitches, which will give you 32 stitches. Then multiply this by the number of strands in the yarn; a four-ply will give you four strands, so multiply 32 by 4. The final figure, 128 in this case, is the number of stitches you will be able to make with a 15-inch length of yarn. The 20 percent gives a margin for mistakes, and for starting and finishing a length. You can work out how many stitches you will need in each color by counting the blocks on the chart.

The "how to" section of each project specifies how much of each color you will need to work the projects on the gauge suggested. However, you can use the method described above to calculate the amount of thread required if you want to work on a finer- or a coarser-gauge canvas or if you choose to use a yarn other than the ones suggested.

NEEDLES

The needles used for needlepoint are blunt and have a large eye. The blunt end slips easily through the holes in the canvas, and the yarn can be threaded easily through the eye. A size-18 needle is correct for working a medium-gauge canvas (10 to 14 meshes per inch). Needles come in different sizes suitable for the differing gauges of canvas available. As with canvas, the higher the number, the finer the needle.

GETTING STARTED

FOLLOWING A CHART

In order to stitch the needlepoint designs in this book, you will need to familiarize yourself with working from a chart. The charts are printed in color, with a key running by the side. The key gives the appropriate yarn numbers required for the project, and each of these numbers is shown with a color-block key that corresponds with the colors on the chart. Each of the colored squares on the chart represents a single stitch.

Before you start, make sure you have all the colored yarns needed to work the design. You will need to sort them onto an organizer or mark them with pieces of paper so that you know which color is which. It is also helpful to cut the skeins into manageable lengths; 15-inch strands are convenient to work with.

PREPARING THE CANVAS

When cutting the canvas, make sure it is at least 2 inches larger all around than the finished design area specified

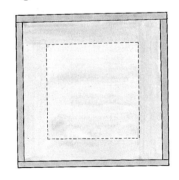

on the key. Bind the edges with masking tape to protect them from fraying. Lay the canvas on a piece of strong paper or board (brown paper is ideal) and draw around the outline of the canvas. While you stitch, your work may become distorted, but you can use this drawing of the original shape as a guide to block your work when you have finished stitching.

Find the center of your canvas by folding it in half and then in quarters. Mark the point where the folds meet with a pencil or a couple of basting stitches. This will be your starting point. It is easier to count the stitches from the chart if you work from the center.

MOUNTING THE CANVAS ONTO A FRAME

You can work without a frame; however, it is not advisable because when working over your lap, you are bound to stretch and distort your work more than necessary. By attaching your work to a frame, you have a firm surface and the design will be easier to stitch.

There are several types of frames from which to choose. These include a scroll frame, a rotating frame, or a stretcher frame. Frames can be fairly costly but are a worthwhile investment because they make stitching so much easier and

STRETCHER FRAME

produce better final results. Ask for advice at your local needlecraft store about the different types of available frames.

The least expensive and most basic, yet practical, is the stretcher frame. Interlocking lengths of wood form the frame. You will need two side pieces and a top and bottom to match the required length and width of your canvas. The canvas is stretched and tacked to the frame. To do this, mark the center of each side of the frame and of each side of the canvas. Tack the canvas to the frame, making sure to match up the center marks on each side exactly. Make sure the canvas is pulled taut. As you tack the canvas in place, keep the tacks symmetrical on each side of the frame to avoid distorting the material.

STITCHES

All the designs in this book use either continental stitch or half-cross stitch. They are easy to work and grow quickly. It is a matter of personal choice which stitch you choose to work because they both look the same from the front. The half-cross stitch covers the horizontal on the back of the canvas, and the continental stitch covers the vertical.

When stitching, work all rows in the same direction to give a uniform appearance to the finished piece. Don't forget that if you turn your work around for any reason, you should make sure your stitches still lie in the correct direction. Try to maintain an even stitch tension throughout.

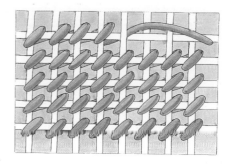

CONTINENTAL STITCH

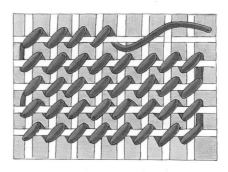

HALF-CROSS STITCH

BEGINNING TO STITCH

Thread your needle and make a knot at the end of your yarn. Starting a few canvas holes ahead of where you want to make your first stitch, take the needle down through the canvas to the wrong side, leaving the knot hanging on the right side. Bring it back up at the point of your first stitch, and start stitching toward the knot. When you reach the knot, cut it off.

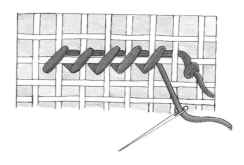

When you finish a length of yarn, take the needle through two or three of the stitches at the back of the work, and then neatly trim the yarn close to the stitches to make a clean and neat finish.

If your yarn becomes tangled while you are stitching, simply let go of the needle, letting it hang from your work. The yarn should twist and allow the tangle to unravel naturally.

FINISHING AND MAKING UP

BLOCKING

When you have finished stitching, the work should be blocked (or stretched) before you make it into the finished article. This will bring back the original shape, which may have been lost during stitching. First, remove your work from the frame. Hold it up to the light to check that there are no missing stitches. Take your original board or brown paper outline of the canvas and attach it with masking tape to a plywood board that is at least 2 inches larger all around. Dampen the back of the worked canvas and place on top of the board or brown paper, wrong side up. Matching the corner of the canvas to the drawn guide, attach the work to the original drawing by gently pulling the canvas back into shape and keeping it in position with tacks hammered in place, about 1 inch apart. Leave this to dry naturally before removing. Badly distorted canvas might need stretching more than once.

WASHING

To wash your work, use a mild detergent and lukewarm water. Do not rub or wring. If you do, you may find the fibers will mat and start to felt. Be gentle, and continue dipping until the water runs clear. Dry your work flat. If you are in any doubt about washing your needlework, seek the advice of a dry-cleaning specialist. This is particularly true for items of clothing, such as the "Seashell Vest" on page 45.

PILLOWS

On average, the pillow size for the projects in this book is 14 inches square. However, some are 16 inches and 18 inches square. In view of this, the following instructions are universal to cover all pillow sizes.

To make a simple pillow, trim the edges of the canvas to leave a $5/8$-inch seam allowance around the stitched design. Cut the backing fabric to the same size as your finished work plus a seam allowance. Place the worked canvas and backing fabric together with right sides facing. Stitch around three sides and part of the fourth, allowing a large enough gap to insert a pillow form. If you buy a slightly bigger pillow form than the size of the pillow and squeeze it inside the cover, it will give a plush, full effect. A feather or down form will produce a softer and more luxurious pillow – well worth the expense after all your hard work at stitching. Turn the pillow cover right side out and slipstitch the edges of the canvas together.

INSERTING A ZIPPER

To make a removable pillow cover for cleaning, insert a zipper into the pillow. Cut the edges off your canvas, leaving a $5/8$-inch allowance around your design. Cut the backing fabric the same width as your canvas but $1 1/4$ inch longer. Cut the backing fabric in half. With wrong sides together, stitch these two pieces with a $5/8$-inch seam at each end only, leaving a gap $7/8$ inch longer than the zipper. Baste the zipper opening and press open.

Fold the seam allowance on one piece by $3/8$ inch and press it firmly. Place it along the edge of the zipper. Pin, baste, and stitch through the fabric and zipper.

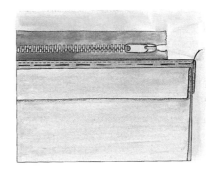

Open out the fabric with the right side facing you and the zipper lying flat underneath. Pin, baste, and stitch the second zipper edge through all the layers. Remove all basting and open the zipper.

Machine-stitch around the four edges, allowing a $5/8$-inch seam. Trim and finish the seams, either with a zigzag stitch or by oversewing.

Turn your pillow to the right side and put your pillow form through the zipper opening.

BOLSTER

To turn your stitched canvas into a bolster, all you will require is lightweight muslin, backing fabric, zipper, and stuffing or batting.

To insert the zipper, follow the instructions above.

Cut two circles in the backing fabric. Their circumference should be the same as the length of the canvas and that of the backing fabric, minus the $1 1/4$ inches that have been allowed for the seams.

With wrong sides together, using a $5/8$-inch seam, sew the canvas and backing fabric together along the long seam. You should now have a tube of fabric. Open the seam and press flat. Open the zipper. With right sides together, pin, baste, and stitch the circles, one to each end of the tube. Finish the edges.

Turn the cover through the zipper opening.

To make a bolster pillow form to fit your bolster cover, cut the muslin to the same size as the tube. Sew the long ends together using a $\frac{5}{8}$-inch seam allowance. Cut two end

circles. Pin, baste, and stitch one end circle to the tube, with right sides together.

Before attaching the second circle, which will be the other end, fill the tube with stuffing. Make sure it is firmly stuffed. Join the second circle and finish edges.

WALL HANGING

To turn your stitched canvas into a wall hanging, you will need backing fabric (upholstery fabric), 2-ounce batting, a wooden dowel, and decorative cord or braid.

Cut the edges off the two long sides of the canvas, leaving a $\frac{5}{8}$-inch border. Cut a piece of backing fabric the same size as the canvas.

Cut a piece of batting slightly smaller than the canvas and baste the batting to the wrong side of the canvas.

With right sides together, sew the backing fabric to the canvas along the side seams. Turn to the right side. Turn under $\frac{1}{4}$ inch at the top and bottom edges. Stitch.

Cut two pieces of dowel 2 inches longer than the bottom edge of the work. Turn under the top and bottom $1\frac{1}{2}$ inches. Stitch, leaving a gap wide enough to feed the dowel through. Thread the dowel through the top and bottom of your work. Attach the cord or braid to each side of the top dowel for hanging.

VEST

To make the needlepoint vest into a garment, you will need fabric for the back (a dupion silk is recommended for a really luxurious finish), fabric for lining, buttons, a bias strip of lining fabric for piping and rouleaux, and piping cord. You will also need the following pattern pieces: stitched front pieces, one left, one right; vest back; pair of front lining pieces; and back lining. Cut the fronts from the stitched canvas, leaving $\frac{5}{8}$ inch all around each piece. Cut front lining pieces the same size.

Cut the back from the pattern on a fold. If you need to adjust the size of the vest, add or take in the extra at the center back. Remember that if you add to the fold, add only half of what you need. Cut the lining to the same size, adding an extra $\frac{7}{8}$ inch at the center back. Cut 2-inch-wide lengths of bias in the lining fabric, joining them together on the cross.

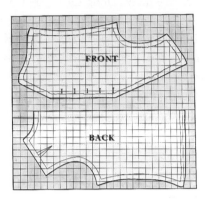

Sew the darts at the shoulders on both the back and the back lining. Sew the front panels to the back with their right sides together. Then sew the front lining to the back lining with their right sides together.

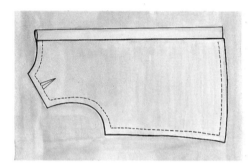

Make a $\frac{3}{8}$-inch pleat at the center back of the lining. Baste it at the top and bottom and press.

Measure around the armhole. Cut two bias strips this length plus $1\frac{1}{4}$ inches. Join them together using a $\frac{5}{8}$-inch seam. Press the seam open. Attach it, right sides together, around the armholes. Stagger the seam and turn the bias to the wrong side. Baste through the vest and the facing on both armholes.

Take a 14-inch bias strip and 14 inches of piping cord. Turning the end under, hand-stitch the bias strip tightly around the cord. Then cut this piped strip into five 2-inch lengths.

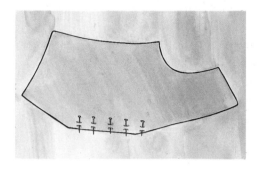

Evenly space five marks along the right-hand side of the center front, starting below the "V." Take each of the piped strips, fold in half, and position at these marks, with the raw edges against the center edge of the vest. Baste each of these in position.

Measure around the edges and cut a bias strip to this length plus 1¼ inches. Cut piping the same length. Fold the bias strip in half around the piping cord. Baste firmly against the edge of the cord.

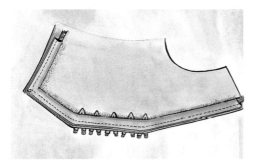

With the piping facing away from the seam, pin, baste, and stitch the piped strip all around the edge of the vest.

Turn the seams under so that you can see the piped edges. Trim into the seams and corners so that the vest lies flat. Baste around the vest inside the seamline and then press. Turn under ⅝ inch around the edge of the lining. Press the lining. Fit the lining to the inside of the vest. Pin, baste, and hand-sew in place.

Sew buttons to the left-hand side, making sure they match the position of the buttonholes. Take out any remaining basting stitches.

MOUNTED PANEL

To turn your stitched canvas into a mounted panel, you will need acid-free board, pins, strong thread, and 4-ounce batting.

Cut a piece of board slightly larger than the finished needlepoint and a piece of batting slightly smaller than this piece of board. Place the finished work right side down on a clean, flat surface, with the batting positioned centrally over the design area. Place the piece of board on top.

Turn one long side of the canvas over the board and pin at intervals along the edge, making sure that the work is sitting in the middle of the board. Holding the work taut, pin along the opposite edge.

Thread a needle with strong thread. Working from side to side and starting at the center, lace the two edges together. Pull the thread taut.

Repeat this process on the top and bottom edges, folding the corners carefully. Tie off the strong thread to finish.

FRAMED PICTURE

To turn your stitched canvas into a framed picture, you will need acid-free board, pins, strong thread, 4-ounce batting and a picture-frame mat insert.

Cut a piece of board slightly smaller than the inside of your picture frame, and a piece of batting slightly smaller than the design area of your work.

Place the finished work right side down on a clean, flat surface, with the batting positioned centrally over the design area. Then place the board on top.

Turn one long side of the canvas over the board and pin at intervals along the edge, making sure that the work is sitting in the middle of the board. Holding the work taut, pin along the opposite edge.

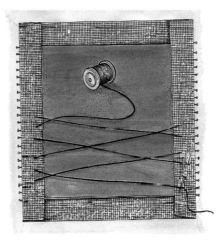

Thread a needle with strong thread. Working from side to side and starting at the center, lace the two edges together. Pull the thread taut. Repeat this process on the remaining edges, folding the corners carefully. Tie the thread off. Place the mat insert inside the picture frame. Place your board-backed work inside the picture frame behind the mat, and insert the backing board into the frame.

AUBUSSON CHAIR CUSHION

To complete this project, you will need ⅜-inch tacks and strong thread.

Leaving 1¾ inches around the edge of the stitched canvas, cut the shape for the seat. Make a double row of stitching around the edge of the canvas to reduce fraying. Run a gathering thread around the edge of the canvas inside the double row. With the stitched piece facing down on a clean surface, place the slip-seat cushion face down centrally on top. Draw up the gathering thread, adjusting the design so that it is positioned where you want it on the slip-seat.

Using a hammer, tack the canvas to the hard underside of the slip-seat. Place the seat on the chair.

CONVERSION CHART

This conversion chart should only be used as a guide
because exact comparisons are not always available.

ANCHOR	DMC	ANCHOR	DMC	ANCHOR	DMC
8002	WHITE	8508	7226	9022	7385
8004	WHITE	8542	7254	9076	7404
8006	ECRU	8542	7260	9078	7406
8012	7745	8542	7459	9080	7428
8020	7484	8542	7790	9214	7362
8040	7472	8546	7264	9256	7422
8054	7739	8588	7711	9274	7584
8058	7504	8604	7244	9282	7679
8060	7455	8608	7243	9324	7493
8060	7506	8610	7243	9324	7724
8162	7360	8686	7798	9382	7491
8168	7946	8714	7284	9382	7492
8196	7606	8714	7292	9384	7724
8204	7107	8792	7306	9386	7463
8220	7110	8820	7802	9388	7513
8234	7875	8824	7296	9388	7525
8258	7124	8824	7591	9392	7514
8258	7851	8824	7930	9394	7416
8264	7169	8838	7288	9402	7492
8264	7447	8838	7297	9442	7452
8306	7851	8882	7327	9442	7453
8366	7760	8882	7701	9446	7174
8368	7196	8894	7692	9448	7174
8368	7354	8896	7323	9504	7171
8368	7759	8898	7927	9524	7918
8400	7758	8904	7339	9602	7448
8400	7961	8906	7999	9622	7840
8412	7202	8924	7860	9674	7624
8414	7204	9002	7542	9678	7234
8418	7205	9020	7541	9768	7624

SUPPLIERS

TAPESTRY YARNS

Anchor Tapisserie:
Susan Bates Inc., P.O. Box F., Route 9A, 212 Middlesex Avenue, Chester, Connecticut 06412, U.S.A.

Coats Paton Leisure Crafts Group, McMullen Road, Darlington, County Durham DL1 1YQ, England.

Appleton Bros. Ltd.:
American Crewel and Canvas Studio, P.O. Box 453, 164 Canal Street, Canastota, New York 13032, U.S.A.

Thames Works, Church Street, Chiswick, London W4 2PE, England.

DMC Creative World:
DMC Corporation, Port Kearny Building # 10, South Kearny, New Jersey 07032-0650, U.S.A.

Pullman Road, Wigston, Leicester LE8 2PY, England.

Paternayan Ltd.:
J.C.A. Inc., 35 Scales Lane, Townsend, Mass. 01469, U.S.A.

EHRMAN

U.K.:
Ehrman, 14-16 Lancer Square, Kensington Church Street, London W8 4EP

U.S.A.:
Ehrman, 5 Northern Boulevard, Amherst, New Hampshire 03031

Canada:
Pointers, 1017 Mount Pleasant Road, Toronto, Ontario M4P 2MI

Australia:
Tapestry Rose, P.O. Box 366, Canterbury 3126

New Zealand:
Quality Handcrafts, P.O. Box 1486, Auckland

France:
Armada, Collange, Lournand, Cluny 71250

Germany:
Offerta Versand, Brunecker Str. 2a, D–6080 Gross-Gerau

Italy:
Sybilla, D & C S.p.a. Divisione Sybilla, Via Nannetti, 40069 Zola Predosa

Spain:
Canvas and Tapestry, Costanilla de los Angeles 2, 28013 Madrid

Belgium and Holland:
Hedera, Diestsestraat 172, 3000 Leuven

Switzerland:
Bopp Interieur AG, Postrasse 1, CH - 8001 Zurich

Sweden:
Wincent, Svearvagen 94, 113 50 Stockholm

Finland:
Novita, P.O. Box 59, 00211 Helsinki

Denmark:
Designer Garn, Vesterbro 33A, DK 9000 Aalborg

Iceland:
Storkurinn, Kjorgardi, Laugavegi 159, 101 Reykjavik

Argentina:
Vickimport SA, 25 de Mayo 596, Sp, (1002) Buenos Aires

143

ACKNOWLEDGMENTS

Thanks to:	For:
Vivienne Wells	Commissioning the book
Brenda Morrison	Art direction
Zöe and Tim Hill	Some great pictures
Carole Keegan	Typing skills
Ethan Danielson	Sorting out the charts
Nic Barlow	Portrait photography
David & Charles	Footing the bill
Ruth Gill Interiors 15 Topsfield Parade, London N8 8PU Tel: 0181 340 6300	Chaise longue, vase, stand candelabra, and yellow pillows on page 26

And special thanks to:	For:
Kaffe Fassett	A partnership of nearly 20 years, building this business

INDEX